"Canadians may eventually feel that the major decisions are being made outside of Canada. Then they may wish to participate in these decisions, and the ultimate cost of the Free Trade Agreement may be paid; the loss of our nationhood..."

"The Free Trade Agreement serves the leaders of big business. They were its motivators and will be its chief beneficiaries."

"No one would object to greater freedom of trade in goods,...We object, rather, to what got appended in the process."

"Canadian negotiators, could be regarded as extremely naive, in giving away control over vast areas of our national life..."

"...Perhaps this represents priorities other than those of the average Canadian."

Yes, Canada Has A Choice

Marjorie Montgomery Bowker
B.A., LL.B., LL.D.

Published by
Voyageur Publishing
(An independent Ottawa-Hull, publishing company)

Cover Concept and Design by Kim Ford.
Editing by Sean Fordyce and Elspeth Butterworth.
Production Coordination by George McKenzie.

For information write:
Marjorie Bowker,
c/o Voyageur Publishing,
82 Frontenac Street, Hull, Québec J8X-1Z5

ISBN: 0-921842-00-7

Printed in Canada
by Tri-Graphic, in Coordination with Gemm Graphics

On Guard For Thee

An independent analysis, based on the actual text of
The CANADA-U.S. Free Trade Agreement

Prepared by
Marjorie Montgomery Bowker
B.A., LL.B., LL.D.

Voyageur Publishing,
82 Frontenac Street, Hull, Québec
(819) 778-2946

Table of Contents

V Energy

VI Alberta's Energy Situation

VII Agriculture

VIII Services And Temporary Entry

IX Investment And Financial Services

X Canada's Social Programs

XI Other Provisions

Foreword

What impelled me to undertake this analysis were widespread comments from even the most educated Canadians that they do not understand what the Free Trade Agreement is all about. Not one in a thousand Canadians has read it, and little wonder, when it is so massive, complex, and intricate.

My aim has been to provide a descriptive commentary in sufficiently abbreviated form so as to enable all Canadians to formulate their own opinions.

The original mimeographed version was produced independently without a sponsor or outside funding. It began without bias, and with a willingness to accept any conclusions that emerged from the study.

The original version of July 1988 was widely circulated largely through the efforts of individual readers. This version is augmented through further reading and study. I will be accepting no remuneration by way of royalties or otherwise from this publication.

The Free Trade Agreement is bigger than this book. What is presented here is complete, but not exhaustive. Included, are the most important points on which any conclusions are based. It is my hope that this book will provide information to assist Canadians in formulating their own opinions.

Marjorie M. Bowker
B.A., LL.B., LL.D.

October 14, 1988
Edmonton, Alberta

Publisher's Note

This book has been edited only with the aim of making the text easier to read and for reference purposes. This includes a reorganized Table of Contents. Otherwise the manuscript is reproduced almost as it was received.

The editors applaud this publication as the beginning of a much needed debate on issues important to the future of this country. We appreciate the author's courage and efforts to ensure that these issues are discussed on a level all Canadians can participate. Due to a lack of information and discussion, a small group of people make important decisions for us with little or no public participation. Hopefully this will change. Both the author and the publishers will consider our objectives reached if a more vigorous discussion of the future of Canada will result from the publication of this book.

The Free Trade Agreement deals with much more than Free Trade; it deals with the future of this country. Since it has been negotiated between two governments of similar outlook, one can only expect that it represents a particular set of priorities and vision for the future. When hearing comments from people on how good or bad this deal is for Canada we must remember that these people are each talking of their own vision of Canada. One must examine closely the sources of these opinions and make a judgment on whether the opinion agrees with our individual vision of a future Canada. Only then can a person decide if this deal is good for them and their Canada.

It is important to separate the actual facts from the working philosophies of those who speak out on Free Trade. We must also be careful to recognize propaganda from the truth at a time when there is a great deal of the former.

Finally, an author's credentials must be based on not just knowledge and experience, but also on how much the speaker has in common with the interests of the listener.

Mrs. Bowker's credentials cannot be questioned. She has experience in law and Canadian life; she has witnessed and aided in the individual's struggle to survive in the most basic of units-the family. Unlike most speakers on Free Trade, she has nothing to gain from supporting either side, and no firm political loyalties to follow. She speaks for all of us and we can trust her.

We at Voyageur Publishing, hope that you will find this book informative and stimulating. Whether you agree or disagree, the opinions expressed in this book are worth hearing.

Voyageur Publishing encourages anyone with a manuscript dealing with national issues to contact us. We would like to hear from you.

Kim Ford and Sean Fordyce
Publishers

October 11, 1988
Hull, Québec.

Acknowledgements

The author and publisher gratefully acknowledge the invaluable assistance of the following people:

Mr. Viggo Kanstrup, Ottawa manager of Print 2000
    For mimeographing and distributing in the Ottawa
    area several thousand copies of the original version.
Mrs. Honey Ray, Calgary.
    For arranging through business persons in Calgary
    the mimeographing of the original version and
    distributing these copies through southern Alberta.
The Pro Canada Network
    For assistance in the wider distribution of this
    book.
Campus Copy Services, Edmonton
    For speed and efficiency in duplicating the first
    200 copies of the original version.
Kevin McFarlane, Lasercomp Solutions, Ottawa.
    For providing the equipment used to prepare and
    edit the text of the manuscript.
Yves St -Jean, Caisse Populaire de Hull,
    For advice and assistance from the beginning.
George McKenzie, of GEMM Graphics, Gloucester,
    For technical assistance in printing, and faith in the
    projects of Voyageur Publishing
Ray Flansberry, of TLC Courier,
    Voyageur's regular courier service.
Penny Croll, Aylmer.
    For encouragement and assistance given to the
    publishers over the past year.
Also the families of the author and publishers who have
encouraged and helped in so many ways.

Introduction

My initial reason for undertaking a study of the Free Trade Agreement was to educate myself. Like many Canadians, I had become bewildered and confused because of a lack of information made available to the public. Perhaps, I said to myself, if I were to take the time to study it, with the benefit of my legal background, I could clarify my own thinking, and shed some light for others. What began as a quest for self-enlightenment, escalated into something much more than a cursory summer pastime. Little did I know the magnitude of the task I was undertaking.

My first problem was to obtain a copy of the full text of the agreement, not just edited government propaganda. This proved far from easy. However I am grateful to the law librarian at the University of Alberta for lending me the only copy available there at the time. This was early June.

With the Agreement in hand, I set to work at my desk in my home in Edmonton. I read all 1100 pages of it, working eight hours a day for four weeks; reading, analyzing, and writing. What first convinced me to do this, was a sense of concern about the implications of the Agreement for Canada. Had I not sensed a concern of some kind, I would not have abandoned the lawn chair in my garden, for the desk in my study.

I would have willingly dismissed the initial misgivings that motivated me, if my study had justified a more favorable conclusion. Instead, as my work progressed, my apprehensions deepened leading me to the broad conclusion that those who know little about the Agreement support it, while those who have studied it are opposed.

I began and ended my study as a supporter of freer trade. I ended as an opponent of this particular Free Trade Agreement.

I am sometimes asked if I have any political affiliations. My answer is that depending on the issues, I have voted at one time or another, for each of the three national parties (at provincial or federal levels) and once for the Social Credit party during its 36 years in office in Alberta.

In embarking on this study, I had two advantages. The first was time, as I am now retired. The second was a measure of legal expertise, having spent much of my life wrestling with legal concepts as a lawyer and judge. Without the latter, the task would have been hopeless.

By July 15 I had completed a 58-page analysis which I typed myself. Then I had 60 copies duplicated at a nearby copy center. Readers were urged to circulate it as widely as possible with the liberty to make duplicate copies. On July 20, I began mailing out copies, each with a covering letter, to federal and provincial politicians across Canada, professional associations, labour groups, journalists, and private citizens. With that accomplished, I expected that I could return to making muffins in my kitchen. However this was not to be, and by the end of September those muffins remained unbaked.

It all began when Jim Coutts, a well-known Toronto columnist, featured my analysis in the Sunday edition of The Toronto Star. This was July 31, 1988, in an article entitled "Former Judge Sees Flaws in the Free Trade Agreement". He told me later this article brought more responses than he had received from any of the hundred columns he had previously written. In response to requests for copies, he and The Toronto Star, mailed out one hundred and eighty copies of my analysis.

Meanwhile, at my home in Edmonton, I was receiving telephone calls from all over Canada asking for copies. One was from a farmer near Stratford, Ontario who wanted to duplicate hundreds of copies for distribution to farm groups. I ordered another forty copies for my own use from the local copy center and continued providing them at no charge to all who requested them. My costs were about $3.00 for printing and $1.48 for postage. I have not accepted any money for work or expenses related to this study. When the lady at the post office appeared curious about my bulk mailing to politicians across the country, I gave her a complimentary copy.

About this time, a kindly lady from Calgary, a widow and senior citizen, named Honey Ray, known for her interest in public affairs, phoned offering to handle distribution in the Calgary area. She began by persuading Calgary businesses to donate copying services, and then distributed these copies to about one hundred persons throughout southern Alberta. I have yet to meet her.

During all of August I continued reading everything I could lay my hands on concerning the vast subject of Free Trade. On August 31, 1988, a column appeared in the Ottawa Citizen by Roy MacGregor under the heading "She's a Free Trade Thinker for the Average Citizen". It sparked such a response that the demand for copies of my analysis became overwhelming. He said later that he had never received such a landslide of interest from any previous column. He wrote this note to me:

> Little did I know when I finished this column that the Citizen would receive 1000 calls, 300 of which got through to me. It meant I couldn't even write a column for two days. You have touched a national nerve, Madam Justice!

On August 31, 1988, the Edmonton Journal ran a lead editorial commending my analysis, followed two days later by a news report. On September 6, 1988, the Ottawa Citizen published another commentary, this one by columnist Marjorie Nichols entitled "Canadians are Hungry for Facts on Trade Deal", in which she stated:

> She (Bowker) has taken this complicated document...and reduced it to a layman's level with a clarity of language to make any ink-stained wretch drool. These are, of course, exactly the qualities that distinguish great judicial opinions: clarity of thought, language and reason... Bowker, with true judicial

impartiality declares her personal interest. It is, simply, to spread enlightenment... I think that Marjorie Bowker is what ordinary Canadians have been looking for: an impartial source who can assist them in making one of the most important decisions of their voting lives.

By early September, when circulation of my analysis became greater than I could handle, I received a telephone call from Viggo Kanstrup who operates a small print shop on Bank Street in Ottawa. He offered to do photocopies and make them available at a cost of $4.00 by mail or pick-up. During the first week he received over one hundred requests a day. By the end of September he had distributed over two thousand copies.

Requests for radio interviews and television appearances began pouring in, many of which I accepted. These are listed in the section titled Media Responses.

On Sunday, September 18, 1988, the Edmonton Journal ran a front-page news feature entitled "Free Trade Fallout 'Flatters' Retired Judge" by staff writer Sherri Aikenhead and a profile feature entitled "Bowker's Zeal Hasn't Waned".

During a holiday visit to Ottawa in Mid-September to attend the christening of our newest grandchild, I received a telephone call from Sean Fordyce who operates a small independent publishing business in Hull, Quebec under the name Voyageur Publishing. He told me his partner Kim Ford and himself have had a long interest in publishing material on national issues, and asked if they could convert my "home-made" copies into a more durable form and reproduce thousands of copies for sale at a low cost. While in Ottawa, I had two lengthy discussions with him, one with George McKenzie, their production coordinator. On September 20, 1988, I entered into a contract giving Voyageur publishing and distribution rights, while retaining the copyright myself. I am declining any royalty payments on the sale of the book or reimbursement for earlier expenditures. The publisher has responded by keeping the cover price below normal market levels.

We agreed on an expanded version of the original, to include not only this introductory commentary, but also the Federal Government's rebuttal of my Analysis, and my response to it. In addition there are two new sections. The first is entitled "Highlights of Major Concerns" which is a capsule conclusion of the complete treatise. The second is a sample of commentaries which have appeared in various newspapers across Canada. I have made alterations and additions to the original part of the manuscript as new information became available.

My wish for this book, is that it will inspire people to read, think, talk, and even prepare commentaries of their own, so that all Canadians can become participants in the national debate which is of vital importance to the future of our country.

Marjorie M. Bowker
Edmonton, Alberta
October 3, 1988.

Editor's Note:
The following twelve sections, are an updated version
of the original manuscript which was photocopied and
circulated under the name:
**What The Free Trade Agreement Means to
You and to Canada.**

I Background To The Free Trade Agreement

How it came about, What is it? Do We need it?

For 16 months during 1986-7, Canadian and American negotiators were engaged in on-going talks over Free Trade. The American deadline for reaching an agreement was October 3, 1987.

A few days before the deadline, Canada's Chief Negotiator, Simon Reisman, walked out of the talks, saying the two sides were too far apart for any hope of an agreement. Days later, The Minister of International Trade, Pat Carney, and Finance Minister, Michael Wilson, flew to Washington, D.C. At the eleventh hour a deal was struck. They announced that overnight an agreement had been reached.

Two months later the text of the Agreement was released, allowing just three weeks before it had to be signed by President Reagan and Prime Minister Mulroney. When it was signed on January 2, 1988, few Canadians knew what it contained.

By September 1988, it had been approved by the United States Congress and was awaiting approval by the Canadian Senate. It is scheduled to come into effect on January 1, 1989.

The Free Trade Agreement (also referred to as "the FTA") is probably the most sweeping and complex document that has ever confronted Canadians. It is not surprising that few people have seen it, fewer still have read it, and still fewer say they understand it. Its content deals as much with economic and commercial matters as it does with Free Trade.

Already 80% of trade between Canada and the United States is free of tariffs and duties. Therefore The Free Trade Agreement's tariff removal clauses deal with only the remaining 20% of our trade.

Questions to ask:

- Are we giving away too much for the sake of this remaining 20%?
- Should Canada's economic future be tied to the United States, which has become the world's greatest debtor nation?
- Would it be better to expand trade on a more global basis, especially with the Asian Pacific region, which is potentially the greatest growth market of the future?

Canada is already a member of GATT (General Agreement on Tariffs and Trade), which is an international agency with ninety-six member countries. Its purpose is to promote trade on a global basis. It has been operating for over forty years, during which time it has reduced visible trade barriers on industrial goods from 40% to 5%.

The Canada-United States Free Trade Agreement acknowledges GATT and asserts that its provisions continue in force. Many of the FTA's provisions go far beyond the Gatt into areas that potentially affect our future sovereignty. If these additional steps were not considered significant, one would question why other countries have not accepted them into the Gatt.

Canada's Past History of Free Trade

The subject of Free Trade with the United States is not new to Canadians. In 1911, the Liberal government under Sir Wilfrid Laurier introduced a Free Trade bill with the United States. The opposition forced an election and the government was defeated. Now, seventy-seven years later, the issue has been revived.

Mr. Brian Mulroney, when campaigning for the Progressive Conservative leadership in 1983, was asked his views on Free Trade with the United States. His reply was that it would "spell disaster for Canada". In the 1984 federal election, he, External Minister Joe Clark and Finance Minister Michael Wilson all campaigned against Free Trade. Only John Crosbie favored it.

Voters in the 1984 election had no reason to assume that a vote for the Tories was a vote for Free Trade, in fact the opposite was true.With a Federal Election called for November 21, 1988, the Free Trade Agreement will be one of the issues before the electorate.

Not only has Canada witnessed a reversal in government attitude towards Free Trade, but also a shift in position of the corporate sector. In 1975 when the Economic Council of Canada proposed Free Trade in its report entitled "Looking Forward", the business community had a negative response to what it perceived as the potential risk of destruction of Canada's manufacturing industry.

Today's all-out endorsement of Free Trade by corporate Canada is sudden. American multi-nationals and Canadian conglomerates are the strongest supporters of Free Trade, while labor is one of its strongest opponents.

Canadian and American Trade Positions

Canada's world trade has been running at a surplus of $800 million per month for the year ending in May 1988. This works out to an annual trade surplus of $9.6 billion.

In contrast, for the month of May 1988, the United States had a world trade deficit of $9.8 billion. In other words a one-month U.S. deficit exceeds Canada's yearly surplus.

As for trade between our two countries, Canada had a trade surplus over the United States for the first four months of 1988 amounting to $4.722 billion (Statistics Canada, June 15, 1988).

Canada is consequently in a favored position over the United States in terms of both World trade and Canada - U.S. trade.

Canada and the United States are already each other's biggest customers, buying and selling $150 billion worth of goods and services annually. In the light of this fact, it is pertinent to ask: Who needs the Free Trade Agreement most? Who will benefit most?

That the United States sees itself as the victor in the Free Trade deal is apparent from an article in the New York Times It states that Canadian tariffs against American imports are "at least twice as high" as U.S. tariffs against Canadian imports. It then quotes an American professor of International Economics, who speaks of the Free Trade Agreement as follows:

> Most members of Congress realize it is a good deal for the American economy to remove the relatively major barriers that Canada has against American trade. (New York Times, June 5, 1988,"News of the Week" section, p. 4).

Is it far-sighted for Canada to be making trade commitments to the United States at a time when all indicators show that the United States is declining as the economic world leader? Several highly reputable Americans have discussed this decline:

> - Lester Thurow, Dean of the Sloan School of Management at M.I.T.states, that in 1945 the United States accounted for about 75% of the world GNP. By the 1980's, this was down to 22%; that the United States is borrowing $200 billion a year from world capital markets to cure its budget deficit; that it is now the "world's largest debtor nation".
> - Patrick Moyhihan, New York Senator, says that if present trends continue, the United States national debt will reach $13 trillion by the year 2000.
> - James Schlesinger of the Center of Strategic and International Studies in Washington, D.C. speaks of the "dramatic shift of the United States from a great creditor nation to the world's largest debtor" adding that "the United States is no

longer economically a predominant power"
(New York Times, June 19, 1988).

Japan has now exceeded the United States in its
Gross National Product. At current growth rates, Japan
is expected to surpass the United States within 10 years
as the world's largest economy (Maclean's July 4,
1988).

The World Economic Conference held in Toronto in
June evoked this comment from reporter Art Pine for the
Los Angeles Times: Contrasting that event with previous
summits, he stated, "In the early 1980's, the United
States was able to dominate these summits, but now its
influence is on the wane". It is not surprising that
Wayne Easter, former President of the Farmers' Union
of Canada, asked the question "Should Canada tie itself
to a falling star?"

The enormous economic shift to Japan and away
from the United States, the apparent slow-down of
productivity in North America, and the resultant decline
of American influence in world economy raises this
question for Canadians to ponder: Should our priority
be in closer trade ties with the United States, or on a
broader scale, particularly with countries of the Asian-
Pacific region, which is evolving as the future zone for
world trade?

The United States Omnibus Trade Bill

Officially known as "The Omnibus Trade and
Competitiveness Act", this is a 1,200 page document
passed by the American Congress on August 3, 1988.
Under it, the United States can impose mandatory
penalties against any country which trades "unfairly"
with the United States. The definition of what
constitutes "unfairly" is to be decided entirely by
American law.

One of the reasons for Canada negotiating the
Canada-U.S. Free Trade Agreement was to insure that
imports from Canada would not be subject to these

punitive sanctions which will be applied to all other trading partners of the United States.

However, the Omnibus Trade Bill, as passed by Congress, contains no exemption for Canada. Indeed it states that the Omnibus Trade Bill will take precedence over the Canada-U.S. Free Trade Agreement. This means that Canada's overall trade position with the United States is no different with the Free Trade Agreement than it would be without it (with respect to sanctions and secure access to the American market). Canada, along with America's other trading partners will be vulnerable to these severe new protectionist measures.

It is occasionally heard that the Omnibus Trade Bill when passed by Congress was watered down so that its effect on Canada would be minimal. However, it has been considered serious enough that protests have been filed against it through GATT by Japan, Korea and the European Economic Community.

Government Propaganda on Free Trade

Publicity from the Federal Government on the Free Trade Agreement extolled its benefits. The government had spent $14 million by the end of March 1988 on promotional materials; including pamphlets, brochures, and video tapes. Yet half a million copies of this material became outdated and ended up in the shredder. In June the government asked for, and received, a further $10 million, for a total of $24 million spent on publicity to promote Free Trade. Obviously no other organization or political party can compete with this level of expenditure.

Advertisements bearing the logo of the External Affairs Department began appearing in August in several newspapers across Canada, containing testimonials by various Canadians attesting to the benefits of the Free Trade Agreement. At least one reader found these ads an offensive use of public funds (Letter to the Editor, Edmonton Journal, October 2, 1988). A Winnipeg business women Meghan Grey, whose photograph and

On Guard For Thee

testimonial appeared in one of these ads, denied she had given permission (News release, August 1988).

Name-calling has been a frequent weapon directed against opponents of Free Trade. Finance Minister Michael Wilson has called them "Weak-willed and narrow of vision". Prime Minister Mulroney has called them "Fearful and timid of mind". Pat Carney when Trade Minister called them "Wimps". Alberta Premier Don Getty went further and called them "Narrow-minded wimps". When Simon Reisman, Canada's chief negotiator later appeared at public hearings before the House of Commons, he referred to opponents of the Free Trade Agreement as "Nazis".

While there has been no lack of publicity, there has been a decided lack of factual data made available to the public. Journalists in January 1988 were denied access to an array of government documents from seven departments, which were believed to include unfavorable comments on the impact of Free Trade. Some of these were the following:

- Memos to Cabinet on job gains and losses from the Employment Department;
- Records relating to the impact on industrial sectors;
- Policy papers from the Energy Department;
- Documents from the Department of Justice on the dispute-settlement mechanism, and the impact on provincial jurisdiction.

When finally released, these documents were heavily censored (press report, January 20, 1988).

There has been an obvious reluctance on the part of the Federal Government to provide objective material on which Canadians could base an informed opinion. This is perhaps not surprising when International Trade Minister John Crosbie, the principal government salesman for the Free Trade Agreement, freely admitted on June 27 in Montreal that he had not read the entire text of the Agreement and that he did not plan to do so

Some Canadians may feel entitled to something more than this from the chief government advocate of a deal which will fundamentally affect our country's future.

II The Free Trade Agreement

What Does The Free Trade Agreement Say?

The free trade part of the Free Trade Agreement deals only with the remaining 20% of Canada-U.S. trade which is still subject to tariffs and trade restrictions, the other 80% of our trade is already duty-free.

The Agreement provides for the elimination of all trade barriers over a ten-year period beginning January 1, 1989.

Having provided for that, it goes on to list a myriad of items to which some exceptions may apply within different times and under different formulae.

The detailed text of the Free Trade Agreement is immense. It consists of over 1,100 pages, including 195 pages of text which is divided into 8 Parts, with 21 Chapters, as well as voluminous schedules, annexes and algebraic formulae.

It deals with Free Trade in "goods" including everything from grain to meat, dairy products to minerals, plastics to hides and textiles, fabrics, footwear, base metals, machinery, vehicles, optical equipment, energy, lumber, wine and spirits.

It deals with Free Trade in "services". This is movement back and forth of workers connected with enterprises or activities in each other's country, including such services as stenographic, accounting, engineering, architectural, insurance, and brokerage services, real estate, telecommunications, computer services, oil and gas field services, and management.

Temporary entry will be allowed to "business persons" of one country to work in the other country on any enterprise or activity connected with Free Trade. These will include accountants, engineers, architects, doctors, nurses, lawyers, teachers, social workers, journalists, and librarians. They would be exempt from any previous approval procedures, certification or immigration requirements and could remain as long as the enterprise or project lasted, the only requirement being that they are "without the intention of establishing a permanent residence".

The Free Trade Agreement allows for investment in each other's country with virtually no limitation on take-overs. It allows for banks and financial institutions of one country to operate in the other. U.S.-controlled banks operating in Canada will be exempt from certain provisions which apply to other foreign banks.

In regard to natural resources, and in particular the energy fields of oil and gas, Canada is required to supply the United States a fixed proportion of our total supply in times of shortage. There is no obligation for the United States to buy oil and gas from Canada if it can get supplies cheaper elsewhere.

Countervailing and anti-dumping duties are not to be removed, but to be renegotiated over a five-to seven-year period. The risk remains that the United States could declare any of Canada's social benefit programs such as health care, unemployment insurance, pensions, regional development programs, subsidies, government loans, and bank guarantees as "unfair subsidies", and could levy a countervailing duty on Canadian goods entering the United States

The Agreement contains elaborate provisions for the resolution of disputes. While the decisions of panels are said to be "binding" there is nothing to insure compliance or enforcement of such decisions other than retaliation or termination.

Either party can terminate the Agreement on six months' notice. This can be considered a mixed blessing and could react against Canada. For Example, an American threat of termination at an inappropriate time to Canada could become a means of inducing concessions during the important negotiations which will follow the implementation of the Agreement. All of these subjects will be examined in detail in the following pages.

Unfair Subsidies, Countervailing Duties, and Anti-Dumping Laws

Not all barriers to trade are removed by the Free Trade Agreement. Hence there is a need to understand the following terms:

UNFAIR SUBSIDIES - Where Canadian goods are being imported into the United States, it might be alleged that the Canadian producer has had the benefit of an "unfair subsidy". The alleged subsidy might have been financial assistance from the government, a guarantee on a bank loan, a rebate on taxes or royalty reductions, or benefits from a regional development program. Because such benefits reduce overhead costs, some Canadian goods could be exported to the United States and sold at a cheaper price than their own domestic products. To protect their industries, the United States might declare that these subsidies constitute "unfair trade".

COUNTERVAILING DUTIES - These are duties which countries add to the price of goods being imported, to offset or "countervail" the benefits of what are regarded as "unfair subsidies" enjoyed by the other country. If the United States threatens to impose a countervailing duty on Canadian goods entering that country, Canada might come under pressure to eliminate the subsidy. In the past the Canadian government has assisted certain industries to compensate for Canadian inequalities. If this practise were stopped, many business, and even whole industries might fail.

ANTI-DUMPING DUTIES - These relate to price differentials. If a product is sold to another country at a lower price than that charged at home, it is considered "dumping". The importing country could retaliate by imposing a duty to restore the price balance. For example: Saskatchewan, when faced recently with an over-supply of potash and falling world prices, shipped supplies to the United States at a price lower than that prevailing in Canada. The United States called this "dumping" and threatened to impose an anti-dumping duty to equalize the price.

It is important to note that the above duties are not removed under the Free Trade Agreement. This is because present "trade laws" between our two countries will continue for at least five years. They will be re-negotiated, but because duties such as these are so entrenched in America trade practice, there is little likelihood of their removal.

Even without a Free Trade Agreement, there are several recent instances of the United States imposing countervailing duties on imports from Canada:

1. In December 1986 when our two countries were negotiating the Free Trade Agreement, the United States threatened to impose a countervailing duty on Canada's lumber. They alleged it was entering the United States at a cheaper price than domestic lumber because Canadian lumber producers enjoyed an unfair subsidy in the form of reduced stumpage fees. At Washington's request the Canadian government agreed to impose a 15% export tax on Canadian lumber leaving Canada. This tax remains in effect. As recently as June 1988, some Alberta forest-product industries were complaining that this tax was creating problems in their export trade. This is an example of American pressure being brought to bear on Canadian legislation.

2. In May 1988 when the Finance Committee of the United States Senate debated approval of the Free Trade Agreement, it threatened restrictions on imports from Canada of lobster and potatoes, in order to protect American producers. This brought objections from Prince Edward Island claiming a threat to that province's economy.

3. In September 1988 the U.S. Senate, intending to protect U.S. manufacturers from competition, approved legislation to curb imports of textiles and clothing from Canada and elsewhere. Although this legislation could face a Presidential veto, its effect would be to limit increases of Canadian textile exports to the United States to 1% annually. In 1987 these exports were valued at $635 million (Cdn.). Limitations on future exports could represent a significant losses to Canada.

4. Perhaps the most noted case was in 1984 when some fifty allegations of unfair subsidies were raised by American officials against the import of Maritime gound-fish. While most of these challenges were not substantiated, the few that were, resulted in Countervailing Duties.

These samples illustrate the frequency with which challenges of unfair subsidies have been raised in our past trade dealings with the United States. The Free Trade Agreement is not going to change this. In fact, the Bill which has just passed Congress approving the Free Trade Agreement contains a clause allowing the U.S. government to monitor Canada's subsidy programs in search of unfair subsidies on an on-going basis. The results would be reported annually to Congress. Subsidy programs of other countries are not subject to similar scrutiny

The risk of countervailing duties continues under Free Trade. They are a far greater barrier to our trade with the United Stated than the direct tariffs which the Free Trade Agreement is designed to remove. It will require intense bargaining on the part of Canada during the five to seven year negotiating period, if any changes are to be effected.

III Jobs and Consumer Savings

Predictions of Job Creation

Confusing and conflicting claims have been made as to the numbers of new jobs which the Free Trade Agreement will create for Canada.

Pat Carney, when Trade Minister speaking in Charlottetown in October 1987, stated that 250,000 new jobs would be created in Canada. However, the following month Employment Minister Bouchard told the House of Commons that his Department had studies predicting that 500,000 jobs would be lost in Canada when Free Trade comes into effect. After a call from the Prime Minister, he denied there were any such studies (October and November press releases 1987).

The federal Finance Department released a study in February 1988 stating that Free Trade would create 120,000 new jobs in Canada in the first five years (1989-1993). These jobs spread over ten provinces, would amount to 2,400 new jobs for each province per year. Statistics Canada's reports of December 1987 showed 12.2 million Canadians were employed and 2.1 million were unemployed. The prospect of 120,000 new jobs over five years would not appear to make a significant dent in Canada's employment situation.

This figure of 120,000 predicted new jobs should be viewed in the context of another figure, namely that given by Finance Minister Michael Wilson in his budget speech in February 1988, when he said that in the same five year period, the Canadian economy alone will create 1,320,000 new jobs. Thus Free Trade would account for less than one out of ten new Canadian jobs during the first five years of the Free Trade Agreement.

The findings of the Economic Council of Canada, which has been supportive of Free Trade are also relevant. It originally predicted that 350,000 new jobs would be created in the first 10 years of Free Trade. However, in a later report released in April 1988, it had dropped this estimate by 30% to 250,000 new jobs over ten years. This would represent an increase in employment of 1.8%. Two of the members of the Council, one an economics professor, said that even this lower figure is too optimistic. This in-depth study by the Economic Council, which is entitled "Venturing Forth" concludes that although it supports Free Trade, the gains in the Agreement are so small that Canada should not hesitate to pull out of it, even if hit by protectionist measures which were then before the American Congress (Ottawa Citizen, April 13, 1988). For details on these measures see the section on the U.S. Omnibus Trade Bill.

In regard to Alberta, the Council report says it may gain 31,000 more jobs over ten years due to greater access to American oil markets. Jim Horsman, Attorney General of Alberta, presented a government booklet on Free Trade in November 1987. This booklet included the statement that 40,000 new jobs would be created in Alberta. In the revised edition, this figure was omitted.

Accurate forecasts as to job gains or losses are obviously impossible. Originally there was a great spate of glowing employment predictions. However one does not hear so much about these anymore.

Potential Losses of Jobs

The Free Trade Agreement will result in the following job losses for Canadians:

1. Many American branch plants now operating in Canada will become redundant and be closed down. The only reason such plants were established in Canada in the first place was to provide a shelter behind the tariff wall. By having a branch in Canada they were able to sell their products to Canadians without a tariff being added to the selling price. However under the Free Trade Agreement, these tariffs will be eliminated in ten years or less so that a Canadian branch becomes unnecessary. Canadian

customers can be supplied equally well (and from the company's standpoint, often more cheaply) from one plant in the United States. With the closure of Canadian branch plants, many Canadian jobs will vanish.

2. A similar result could occur in regard to the many businesses operating in Canada which are wholly owned by Americans. Though the shift here is not likely to be so immediate, some of these companies will close out their Canadian operation and move to the United States. Once the tariffs are removed they can serve the Canadian market equally well from there. The result will be more job losses for Canadians. Even some Canadian-owned businesses could be lured by greater markets, knowing they will still be able to serve their Canadian customers from the United States.

3. Many branch plants and American-owned companies are located in smaller towns where they are the main industry and chief employer. If the Free Trade Agreement makes it advantageous for theses business to relocate, some of these presently prosperous communities will become welfare-oriented, or even revert to ghost towns because of the lack of alternate employment.

4. The ease of American investment in Canada under the Free Trade Agreement will result in an increase in American take-overs of Canadian businesses (especially the successful ones). Takeovers are said to generally result in an immediate loss of 20% of the jobs of the acquired company. The new American owners may even find it more profitable to move the entire operation to the United States. Without the tariff barriers, it would make more sense to locate near the larger population centres, and ship goods to

Canada. The result would be greater efficiency and lower operating costs for the company. The cost would be more Canadian jobs.

5. Canadians who would have considered starting a business in Canada may find it more advantageous to locate in the United States. With the removal of tariffs, these companies can supply Canadian customers just as easily as if located in Canada. At the same time they would be nearer to large American markets, and have the advantage of lower operating costs than in Canada. Seminars are already being conducted across Canada, some sponsored by the Federal Government to inform and train business people as to how they can locate to their advantage in the United States. Advice is given on such things as American tax laws, employee benefits, and labor unions. New businesses enticed away from starting up in Canada, represent lost jobs out of current forecasts.

There are major incentives for locating a business in the United States rather than Canada, once the Free Trade Agreement comes into effect. The United States generally has lower labour costs. At least nine states do not have a minimum wage law. There are fewer employee benefits to which employers must contribute. Employers in the United States do not have to pay a share of the employees' premiums for health care, unemployment insurance, or pensions. In the United States, only employers whose companies are unionized pay a share of health care premiums. Transportation costs to get goods to the large centres of American Population are much lower. Finally, a milder climate reduces construction costs for new facilities, and cuts down or eliminates certain operating costs such as heating.

The Myth of a Large-Scale Movement of Workers

The remark is often made that Canadian workers will move to the United States and follow the jobs there. While executive and managerial personnel may well do so as their expenses are paid by their company the average worker would find such a move impractical, costly and personally disruptive. These are some reasons:

a) Family ties to an extended family;
b) Community attachment (sometimes life-long);
c) Possible adverse effects on spouse and children;
d) Educational concerns;
e) Housing;
f) No assurance of obtaining work in the United States in competition with American workers;
g) Loss of Canadian health care benefits, pensions, and unemployment insurance;
h) The elusive lure of simply remaining Canadian.

The Myth of Re-Training Programs

Similar considerations apply, for domestic programs for re-training and re-location of workers. Since employment opportunities must match specific skills, no program, however costly, could meet the employment needs of workers displaced as an indirect result of the Free Trade Agreement.

Basic to all these factors are the underlying inequalities which exist between two countries. The wide differences in population size and economic strength work against any fair exchange of our respective labor forces and business operations. Before Canadians base their endorsement of the Free Trade Agreement on optimistic forecasts of new jobs, it would be wise to reflect on these realities.

The Myth of Consumer Savings

The Free Trade Agreement has been touted as a savings bonanza for consumers. The word "free" has tremendous public appeal. Anything with that name must be good.

Predictions of consumer savings must, be tempered by these realities:

a) The largest proportion of remaining tariffs on goods entering Canada is less than 5%. However, on some items of clothing from the United States, it is as high as 25%. The gradual removal of these tariffs over a ten year period will not result in perceptible savings to consumers.

b) Goods purchased in the United States with less than 50% American content are still subject to duty. Many consumer items on sale in the United States come from Korea, Japan, Mexico, China, Hong Kong, and will still be subject to tariffs when sold to Canadians.

c) The largest levy on consumer goods sold in Canada is caused by Federal Government sales tax, which remains intact.

From a government budgetary perspective, the following additional factors are pertinent:

a) The Federal Government is currently spending $30 billion a year in excess of revenue;

b) The estimated loss of income from tariff removal will reach $24 billion by 1998;

c) This loss of revenue must be compensated by income from some other sources, possibly by a value-added tax on goods and services. This is forecast under the Tax Reform Bill, second phase.

Federal Government promotional literature has emphasized consumer savings under the Free Trade Agreement. However, a document of the federal Finance Department dated December 16, 1987 and released to the Canadian Press on August 11, 1988 under the Access to Information Act does not seem to substantiate these claims.

This document suggests the full impact of tariff cuts may not be visible at the check-out counter. The extent of reductions in consumer prices will depend more on what wholesalers and retailers regard as an acceptable profit margins and whether they choose to pass on their savings to consumers.

An added factor is the imbalance in exchange rates between our two countries. Goods imported from the United States will continue to cost more for Canadian consumers even under the Free Trade Agreement.

While there will be some savings for consumers after tariff removal, there has been a tendency to exaggerate their extent.

IV The Effect On Certain Industries

The Textile Industry

The textile-garment industry employs 94,000 workers in Canada and two million in the United States. Wages tend to be lower in the United States because companies there do not have to pay a share of employee benefits as they do in Canada. This means lower production costs in the United States and lower prices on finished garments. Before Free Trade, Canada was able to impose import duties on American textiles entering Canada in order to keep prices high enough for Canadian factories to compete, and thus protect Canadian jobs.

Over the years, in order to encourage Canada's infant textile industry, it has been heavily subsidized by the Federal Government. Under Free Trade, such subsidies would cease. Canada would be flooded with merchandise from the United States at prices which cannot be matched by Canadian manufacturers and as a result smaller firms could be forced out of business. The larger, successful factories could be absorbed by U.S. companies, and moved to the United States where wages are lower and markets larger. This could seriously affect female employment in Canada, as most workers in the textile industry are women. While Canadian consumers may rejoice over cheaper goods from the United States, the cost could be the destruction of this important Canadian industry. Goods from other countries will be still subject to tariffs.

The Wine and Spirits Industries

Of all Canadian industries, wine and spirits stand to be major losers under the Free Trade Agreement, and likely to be hardest hit first. In fact, Ontario's objection to this particular clause has been so strong that its Premier has threatened to reject the Free Trade Agreement altogether because of it.

It has been the practice in Ontario to protect its infant wine industry by adding a mark-up to the price of wines imported from California, so that Ontario wines could compete on the basis of being less expensive. Article 803 of the Free Trade Agreement will eliminate "discriminatory" mark-ups on American spirits "immediately upon the entry into force of this Agreement". The mark up on wine will gradually be eliminated on an annual basis until 1995. Some Ontario wine producers feel this would destroy their industry.

The Federal Government denies any complaints by the wine industry regarding provisions in the Free Trade Agreement. However, a grant of $28 million was made in aid of the British Columbia grape growers. This was announced in the Prime-Minister's Western Canada tour in August 1988. Obviously all is not well, or there would be no need for such expenditures.

The Automotive Industry

Promoters of the Free Trade Agreement frequently refer to the success of Auto Pact as evidence of the benefits of Free Trade. The Auto Pact has been in effect since 1966.

Stated in simplest terms, the Auto Pact is designed to help both countries in the following manner:

a) It works in favor of the United States by removing duties on cars and parts entering Canada from the United States for sale here. This makes the sale price low enough to be competitive; and gives the United States access to the Canadian car market ranked the seventh largest in the world.

b) It works in favor of Canada in that Canada can have its own auto manufacturing industry (albeit in the form of American-owned branch plants). This provides jobs for Canadians largely because of the "safeguard" built into the Pact which requires 60% of production costs (goods and services) to be "Canadian content".

The Autopact cannot properly be described as a Free Trade agreement; rather it is a contract which applies to a specific commodity (autos) on specific terms, only one of which deals with elimination of custom duties. Many people feel that individual contracts of this kind, covering specific commodities would be a better course for Canada to pursue, rather than a comprehensive Free Trade Agreement.

Though the Free Trade Agreement purports to preserve the Auto Pact, it does so in typically obscure language (Article 1001). Also, Chapter 10 on "Automotive Goods" has to be read in conjunction with Chapter 3, "Trade in Goods". The required 60% Canadian content, will become 50% North American content [Chapter 3, Annex 302.2, Rule XVII, Sec.5]. In effect this means that Canada could lose the advantage it has enjoyed under the Auto Pact which has insured that the bulk of supplies and labor used in the auto industry has a domestic source.

The Resource Industries

Article 409 of the Free Trade Agreement has caused this writer a great deal of concern that Canadians have not been made aware of what it says. Yet there is no other legal interpretation that can be given than that outlined below. Article 409 applies to all "goods" literally all our natural resources, including minerals such as copper, lead, nickel, zinc, aluminum, coal. (Oil and natural gas are dealt with later under "Energy").

Like most Articles of the Agreement, it applies to both countries. In respect to Canada, which has by far the larger share of minerals. Article 409 says: If Canada for whatever reason declares a shortage of any of these commodities, we cannot impose a restriction on our exports to the United States unless:

(a) the United States still receives a fixed proportion of our total export shipments of that commodity in relation to our total supply of it;

(b) Canada does not charge a higher price than that charged domestically.

Canadians have repeatedly been told that control of our natural resources is unaffected by the Free Trade Agreement. Yet the above Article makes it very clear that in the event of a shortage our control will be lost in respect to both the proportion of our supplies that we must export to the United States, and the floor price we are entitled to charge.

This severely limits Canada's opportunities to sell any of these resources to other countries at higher than domestic prices at such a time.

V Energy

The New Energy Realities

Trade in "energy" is dealt with in Chapter 9 of the Free Trade Agreement. The term "energy" is broadly defined (Article 901.2). It includes oil and gas, electricity, coal and its derivatives, and uranium.

This analysis will concentrate on oil and gas exports to the United States from Alberta; Canada's main supplier. Though the Alberta government has given its unqualified approval to the FTA provisions on energy, there are some important factors which should be weighed by Canadians, particularly Albertans. The provisions outlined below also apply to other provinces including Ontario, Quebec, and British Columbia which deal in the sale of electricity generated by coal or hydro.

It is clear from the text that sales of Alberta energy to the United States will be subject after a declared shortage to the following restrictions:

1. There will be no "tax, duty, or charge" on exports to the United States which do not also apply to Canadian consumers (Art. 903);
2. Canada's restrictions on exports to the United States are subject to the following conditions:

(a) Canada makes available to the United States a fixed proportion of its total energy supply [Art. 904(a)];
(b) the price at which Canada sells to the United States will be no higher than that charged to Canadian consumers [Art. 904(b)];
(c) there is no disruption to normal channels of supply [Art. 904(c)].

The term "restrictions" includes quotas, licenses, permits, and minimum price requirements - (Art. 908).

A procedure is provided for consultation where one country alleges that regulatory actions of the other results in discrimination (Art. 905). Article 906 permits "incentives" for oil and gas exploration and development in order to maintain reserves. The implications here is that though Canada would be providing such incentives at considerable cost to the economy, United States is not obliged to contribute, though it would be the beneficiary of the results.

Article 907 says that the only justification for Alberta, for example, to restrict oil and gas exports to the United States would be:

- to fulfil a critical defence contract;
- armed conflict involving Canada;
- nuclear threat.

The message from politicians is that the opening of United States markets to imports of oil and gas from Canada will lead to economic growth and prosperity; that industry will expand and jobs will be created. Only close scrutiny of the Agreement itself can determine if such claims are true. Though the energy provisions of the FTA apply equally to both countries, Canadians will be more interested in the impact on Canada. This will be examined under the various headings which follow.

The Effect On Supplies

Article 904(a) is the key provision here. Under it, the United States is entitled to a fixed proportion of Canada's "total supply" of an "energy good". The term "total supply" is defined in Article 909 as "shipments to domestic and foreign users from domestic production, domestic inventory, and other imports as appropriate" - a sweeping coverage of our energy resources from whatever source.

Under the Free Trade Agreement, when Canada declares a shortage, there can be no government legislated reduction in the proportion of Canadian supply of oil and gas going to the United States. If our supplies diminish, the United States will still get a proportion of whatever is left. We must continue to share our short supply with the United States, however small that may be.

In the past, Alberta has always controlled whether its oil and gas went to domestic, or foreign markets. These products, like so many others, were assumed to be a national resource first, and an export commodity second. Until 1987, the National Energy Board required that Canada have a 25-year reserve of gas before exports could occur. This was reduced to 15 years in 1987 and has since been eliminated altogether. The effect of the Free Trade Agreement will be to limit the ability of the National Energy Board to control exports in the future and to assure adequate energy supplies to Canadians. In times of shortage, Canadian customers will have even less because a proportion of the supply will already be allocated for export to the United States.

It may come as a surprise to Canadians that while the United States has preferred rights to our oil and gas, there is no obligation under the Free Trade Agreement for the United States to buy from Canada if there are cheaper supplies elsewhere. This means that Canada's access to American markets will depend on our keeping the price equal, or less than that of either United States or world producers.

We do know, however, that the United States wishes to get all the Canadian oil and gas that it can. It is cheaper than their own production since American producers pay far higher state and federal royalties than their Canadian counterparts, and do not have the same lucrative incentives for exploration and development. For Canada, it means we have to abandon our dream of national energy self-sufficiency, because the FTA commits us to share our oil and gas with the United States even as our reserves run dry.

While many persons are asking if this is not an erosion of provincial resource control, Alberta Premier Don Getty is satisfied with Mr. Mulroney's assurance that it is not. However, if a conflict arises, even a decade from now, it will not be the assurance of a politician, but the wording of the Agreement that will prevail; and the wording of Article 904(a) is clear.

The Effect On Prices

When a shortage is declared, the price we charge the United States for our oil and gas cannot be higher than the price charged to Canadian consumers [Art. 904(b)]. Differential pricing in such circumstances ends under the Free Trade Agreement. In other words, we cannot show preference in favor of our own citizens even with our own resources.

The export price on our oil and gas will be determined as follows:

> (a) Oil - the price on oil will be fixed by OPEC, a cartel of 13 countries (mostly Middle East). Only if they agree to limit production, will the price of oil rise. At their latest meeting held in Vienna in mid-June 1988, they once again failed to reach agreement on this, which means oil prices, such as what Canada will be charging the United States, will remain low. As of late June 1988 oil was trading well below $17 U.S. a barrel. It has fallen even lower since then to $12.60 U.S. per barrel as of October 5, 1988.
> (b) Natural Gas - the price here will be the "continental price", which really means the U.S. market price: i.e. what the United States is prepared to pay and where it can buy its supplies cheapest.

We will have lost our control over price, just as we will lose control over supplies. There will be no more "made in Canada" pricing.

The Effect On Petro-Chemical Industries

American companies, under the FTA, are assured of obtaining Alberta oil and gas in the United States.

Until such a time as Canada declares a shortage, supply and pricing are governed by ordinary market conditions. However, when a shortage is declared, the United States is assured of obtaining Alberta oil and gas at the same price as they would pay for it in Canada. It would therefore be logical and to their advantage to move their refineries and petro-chemical industries out of Alberta, as most are already owned by U.S. multi-nationals, and re-locate them in the United States where they will be nearer to major population markets. It is more cost effective to locate such industries near to consumers than to the source of crude oil. With the departure of these industries from Alberta will go many jobs presently held by Canadians.

The Effect On Future Oil Development

In the immediate years ahead, the oil and gas which Alberta exports to the United States will continue to come from easily accessible sources, that is "conventional oil". This is relatively inexpensive to extract compared to other sources. We do not know how long these supplies will last. One writer has said that the total of Canada's reserves would satisfy less than a year of American consumption. Suffice to say, United States consumption of oil is by far the heaviest of any country of the world. Canadian supplies make up only 4.7% of United States annual consumption.

When our reserves of cheaper conventional oil are exhausted, Canada will have to depend on the development of huge and costly synthetic plants, of which Syncrude is an example. These are enormously expensive, and are only made possible by the injection of huge amounts of government capital.

If one were to project into the future, the sequence of events facing Canada could be as follows:

1) Supplies of conventional oil will gradually become exhausted. This has been projected for the mid-1990's.

2) Even before that happens, Canada will have to restrict production as a conservation measure. This means articles XI and XX of GATT come into play. At that point article 904 of the FTA becomes activated.

3) Once this happens, we must sell to the United States a proportionate share of our remaining supplies at a price no higher than the Canadian price.

4) From this point on, in order to meet even Canada's domestic needs, costly mega-projects will be needed. More and more these will have to be financed by Canadian governments which in turn means Canadian taxpayers.

5) Whatever is produced from such mega-projects will also have to be shared with the United States under the terms of article 904.

This could then become the pattern of the future: Canadians subsidizing American consumers.

While these projections may not be in keeping with those of the government of Canada, the writer is satisfied that they are reasonable and sound.

Advantages to the United States and to Canada

U.S. Advantages:
1. Secure access to Canadian oil and gas after a declared shortage, and at a price no higher than that paid by Canadians (it could even be lower).
2. No obligation to buy from Canada if cheaper supplies available elsewhere.

3. Assurance of a proportionate share of Canadian oil and gas even in times when Canadian consumers are faced with shortages.

President Reagan, when addressing an International Gas Conference in Washington D.C. on June 6, 1988 heralded the Free Trade Agreement "as a means of enhancing the energy security of America". Canadians may well ask if it does the same for them.

Canadian Advantages
1. Access to the U.S. market, which is willing to take all the oil and gas which Canada can supply, provided it cannot get it cheaper elsewhere.

2. Petro-chemical industries, largely American-owned believe that reduced tariffs will boost sales of their products to the United States, and that this will spur industry growth in Canada. Higher (world) prices for Canadians could result in higher profits for petro-chemical industries.

The test for Canadians will be to weigh the relative merits of the energy provisions of the Free Trade Agreement in respect to our two countries. Because of conflicting interpretations of these energy provisions, the writer presents an additional commentary under the section entitled "Highlights of Major Concerns".

VI Alberta's Energy Situation

Alberta's Short Term Gains in Jobs

Increased sales of oil and gas will result in more jobs for Albertans, at least in the short term. However Alberta may not be able to rely on the oil industry to provide jobs over the long term. The New York Times, October 2, 1988, "News of the Week" reports that the world oil export business will not be as significant in the future for these reasons:

1. Oil is becoming more easily supplanted by other sources of energy.
2. Energy-savings strategies have cut deeply into worldwide energy consumption.
3. Industrial countries have accumulated huge strategic reserves against possible future boycotts or shortages.

This may be a sobering thought for a province inclined to rely on oil exports for long term employment. Statistics Canada, as of December 31, 1987, reported that the oil industry supplies 350,000 jobs, compared to the 12.2 million employed persons in Canada. The oil industry makes a relatively minor contribution to overall employment in Canada. The fear for Albertans is that when the supply runs out, so will the jobs.

Alberta Loss of the Ontario Gas Market

Alberta may have gained in exports to the U.S. market, but it is losing the natural gas market of Ontario, Canada's largest consumer. The reason for this loss (as confirmed by a press interview by Alberta Energy Minister Neil Webber on June 21, 1988) is that Alberta's policy is to charge a higher price under a longer-term supply contract which would assure Ontario of greater security of supply. The reason for the higher prices of Alberta producers is provincial royalty charges, which the government is not inclined to reduce. Ontario, on the other hand prefers to buy cheaper gas, even on a short-term basis. In fact, Union Gas of Ontario is building a $1 million pipeline (0.7 km. in length) from Windsor to Detroit to bring in cheaper American gas to Ontario. It is expected to transport 500 million cubic feet a day by November 1988. Construction for this pipeline was approved by the National Energy Board on June 28, 1988. At least two Ontario cities, Sarnia and Chatham, have switched to Saskatchewan for the purchase of natural gas, saving 20% on the Alberta price. This breaks a monopoly Alberta has enjoyed for some thirty years.

Only an economist could say whether the loss of this large Ontario market for Alberta natural gas will be compensated by exports to the United States which Canada can expect to make under the Free Trade Agreement.

VII Agriculture

Agriculture is dealt with in Chapter 7 of the Free Trade Agreement which is by far the longest chapter. While consisting of only 11 Articles, it includes numerous schedules, annexes, appendices and formulae, which in themselves run over 30 pages. In addition, these agricultural provisions incorporate many rules and definitions drawn from outside documents, including:

- GATT - The International Agreement on Tariffs and Trade - which has been making and amending rules governing world-wide trade liberalization for 40 years.
- The "Harmonized Commodity Description and Coding System" which classifies goods under tariff headings, amended from time to time, and published by the Custom Cooperation Council.

If one hoped to fully comprehend the meaning of the Free Trade Agreement provisions on Agriculture, it would be necessary to master these voluminous documents which are outside the Agreement and which could only be grasped by top-level international trade experts. This commentary will concentrate less on details than on the general principles set forth in this Chapter.

It is well known that agricultural subsidies have become a world-wide problem, with billions of dollars being paid out annually to farmers on a global scale. When first developed after World War II, subsidies were meant to increase food production for a war-ravaged world. The incentives granted to farmers led to higher grain production and eventually a world-wide glut, and consequently the present severe drop in grain prices. Despite these disastrous results, no country wants to reduce these subsidies which enable farmers to continue in business. GATT has not been able to address this problem satisfactorily. Indeed President Reagan's hope for their elimination by the year 2000 is now viewed as

On Guard For Thee

overly optimistic.

Nevertheless, the Canada-U.S. Free Trade Agreement has attempted to deal with some aspects of the subsidy problem in the following manner,

1. The primary goal of the Agreement is to work towards the eventual elimination of all agricultural subsidies which distort world trade [Art. 701(1)].

2. The FTA does not abolish subsidies completely, but it does abolish "export subsidies". These are defined as subsidies "conditioned upon the exportation of agricultural goods" (Art. 711). An example of an export subsidy could be: Canada sees a potential for beef exports to the United States, and wishing to take advantage of greater trade, pays Canadian beef producers an extra $2 per kilogram on beef designated for export. This practice would now be prohibited under the FTA as export subsidies are banned and cannot be introduced [Art. 701(2)].

3. The FTA prohibits one country from "dumping" its agricultural products on the other; that is, selling below the cost of production in order to get rid of a surplus [Art. 701(3)].

4. The Free Trade Agreement does not prohibit either country from having export subsidies when trading with third countries, but when doing so, Canada and the United States are expected to take into account any undesirable effect this might have on each other. This is more of an admonition than a command, and nothing is said about how complaints would be handled. An example might be this: In Canada's trade with India, Canadian chicken producers might be subsidized with guaranteed loans on new equipment. While this is not forbidden under the Free Trade Agreement, Canada should consider if such an arrangement might be harmful

to the United States. The United States could, for example, feel obliged to grant similar incentives to maintain a competitive supply for export.

5. There can no longer be reduced transportation rates in Canada on grain shipments for export to the United States through west coast ports. This will require an amendment to the Canadian Western Grain Transportation Act. Reduced rates will remain for shipments heading east through Thunder Bay [Art. 701(5)].

Special provisions follow regarding trade in fruits and vegetables (Art. 702). For twenty years these can be subject to a "temporary duty" which can be applied on either a national or regional basis. This means, for example, that Canada could apply such a duty on imports of fruits and vegetables originating in the United States. Elaborate descriptions follow, including a long list of what is meant by fruits and vegetables, and how the duty is to be calculated.

Article 703 speaks of the elimination or reduction of "import barriers" on agricultural goods. This term is not defined, but such barriers could take many forms. It is expressed as a wish or hope, rather than as a mandatory requirement. Article 704(1) deals with meat exports and forbids "quantitative" restrictions. An example would be, "We will allow in only 1,000 head of cattle over the next two months". Such quantitative restrictions are forbidden on meat and on sugar products (Art. 707). Article 705 deals with the elimination of "import permit" requirements. These arise out of huge government-support programs which prevail in both countries. There is a long list of these (Schedule I being American programs: Schedule 2 being similar Canadian programs). In Canada, government-support programs include such things as:

-payments to farmers under the Agricultural Stabilization Acts (federal and provincial);

-advance grain payments;
-crop insurance;
-transportation;
-research grants.

Because of government-support programs such as these, an "import permit" is required when grain enters the other country. This is really a restriction on trade, and is to be eliminated. When is this to take place? At the point where U.S. government-support programs reach the level of those in Canada? Algebraic formulae contained in annex 705.4 determine a method for calculating when this level is reached.

Article 706 requires Canada to import chicken, turkey, and egg products from the United States up to a certain percentage of our domestic production. An annex defines what these products include. Article 708 deals with agricultural food and beverages, and aims at an "open border" policy. To assist in this process, both countries will work towards the elimination of technical regulations and standards which may in fact be disguised restrictions on trade. The aim will be to harmonize the inspection systems of the two countries. Lengthy schedules and annexes provide a guide as to how this is to be done.

After analyzing the agricultural provisions of the Free Trade Agreement, one is struck with how complicated they all are. In summary, they include:

- Elimination of export subsidies:
- Prohibition against dumping:
- A temporary import duty allowed for twenty
  years on fruits and vegetables:
- Elimination of special rail rates on grain to west
  coast ports:
- Elimination or reduction of import barriers:
- Elimination of qualitative restrictions on meat,
  exports, and sugar:
- Future elimination of import permit require-
  ments relative to government-support programs;

- Canada's acceptance to import chicken, turkey and egg products up to a certain percentage of our domestic production:
- An open-border policy on agricultural goods and beverages by harmonizing inspection and standards systems between the two countries.

Each country perceives benefits accruing to its farmers under the Free Trade Agreement. Wayne Easter, former President of the National Farmers Union, speaking in Edmonton in February 1988, said that American and Canadian farmers are being told different versions of the effect of Free Trade on agriculture. His organization opposes the deal for Canadian farmers.

Some of the concerns that have been voiced by Canadian agricultural producers are:

1. There is no real guarantee that Canada will not be flooded with American grain from suppliers eager to unload their huge surpluses.

2. The Canadian Wheat Board which has served Canadian farmers so long, and so well, might face extinction. It is the exclusive seller of Western Canada's wheat, oats and barley. As such, it accepts grain from all farmers on the same basis: an initial payment at a fixed price per ton. Further payments are added on an equalized basis as the grain is sold on the domestic or foreign market. In contrast, the United States operates under an "open market" system, where farmers compete for the sale and storage of their grain amongst national elevator companies.

3. Transportation subsidies on grain destined for the United States, such as have long been provided under the Grain Transportation Act, could be in jeopardy.

4. Regarding poultry, American producers enjoy a lower per-unit cost and could undercut the price charged by Alberta producers. (Alberta now has a $100 million chicken-product industry which

54   *On Guard For Thee*

could be threatened.) The writer learned of a Regina supermarket selling dressed chicken imported from the state of Georgia, where labor is cheap. The selling price is much below that of Saskatchewan producers. Yet the Free Trade Agreement requires Canada to import these products from the United States up to a certain percentage of our domestic production.

5. While the Free Trade Agreement exempts both countries from each other's meat import laws, hogs continue to be subject to American countervailing duties. These add $10 to the price of every Alberta hog shipped to the United States, making them less competitive

6. Canadian livestock producers can expect to gain new markets for cattle, but increased exports to the United States could leave Alberta packing plants with a shortage of animals for slaughter (Report of the federal Department of Agriculture, March 1988).

The effect of these provisions can be very important to our country, since according to Statistics Canada (May 1988), there are 222,000 persons employed in agriculture throughout the prairie provinces. This is a sizeable part of Canada's working population and it is important that they remain in the farming business.

It is difficult, for this writer at least, to determine if Canadian agriculture will gain or lose under the Free Trade Agreement, other than to say there is no positive proof of benefits accruing to Canada.

VIII Services And Temporary Entry

Trade In Services

Chapter 14 of the Free Trade Agreement deals with Free Trade in services - the first trade agreement in the world to do so on this scale[1]. It would apply where an enterprise owned or controlled in one country is operating in the territory of the other [Art. 1402(7)]. It would allow workers to be brought in to perform a multitude of services connected with that enterprise (Annex 1408), ranging from agricultural, forestry, mining, and construction services; to engineering, architectural, accounting, and management services. These workers are to be accorded "no less favorable" treatment than that accorded national workers (Art. 1402). There is to be mutual recognition of licensing and certification (Art 1402). Special "Sectoral Annexes" set out professional standards for three of the many categories listed, namely, architects, tourism services, and computer and telecommunication services. It is anticipated that more services will develop similar guidelines (Article 1405).

Because of our country is so much smaller, there are likely to be more American enterprises operating in Canada than the reverse, and consequently more employees brought in to provide these services. This could be a particular problem if American-controlled health-care facilities are established in Canada, where owners could bring in their own service personnel to replace jobs which normally go to Canadians, many of

---

[1]Not long ago the United States concluded a limited agreement for trade in services with Israel. The member countries of GATT have consistently refused to include services in their trade talks because of its effect on national employment. However, because of American insistence, it is on the agenda for the next round of talks. It is believed that one reason the United States is anxious to conclude this agreement with Canada is to strengthen its pressure on other GATT members. The United States apparently views its gains in "services" and energy as its greatest triumphs from this agreement with Canada.

On Guard For Thee

subject, it is discussed further in the section titled "Highlights of Major Concerns".

Temporary Entry

Chapter 15 provides for "Temporary entry" of "Business persons" from one country to the other. "Business persons" means persons engaged in some enterprise or activity connected with Free Trade. "Temporary entry" means entry without the intention of establishing a permanent residence, though no time limit is specified as to how long such persons can remain. While these measures, like most others, are reciprocal, these comments will focus on the Canadian perspective and discuss temporary entry into Canada of American business persons involved in activities arising from Free Trade.

The many purposes or functions for which such persons could enter Canada are listed in Schedule I of the Annex to Chapter 15 They include services relating to:

-Research and design;
-Manufacture and production;
-Marketing and sales;
-Custom brokers;
-After-sales service (installation, repair, and maintenance);
-General service personnel (including professional, managerial and supervisory);
-Computer specialists;
-Insurers, bankers, brokers;
-Public relations and tourism personnel.

Professional persons who can be granted temporary entry in connection with such enterprises are set out in Schedule 2. There are forty five in all and and include the following:

accountants, engineers, scientists, physicians, dentists, nurses, veterinarians, psychologists, architects, lawyers, teachers, economists, social workers, journalists, and librarians.

All such personnel will be granted entry into Canada without the usual immigration requirements, prior approval procedure, or labor certification

This might well cause concern for professional societies in Canada. Mr. Harvey Bliss, President of the Ontario Branch of the Canadian Bar Association, has expressed concern over these provisions in relation to the legal profession ("National", February 1988). He said that American companies engaged in lengthy enterprises in Canada (any transaction "covered" by Free Trade) could bring in their American lawyers to advise them throughout the full term of the project, which may go on for several years.

This means that the Canadian public would be dealing with American lawyers not trained in the Canadian legal system. It would be particularly difficult in negotiating contracts in Quebec requiring a knowledge of Quebec's Civil Law. A report from the Canadian Press dated August 8, 1988, containing an interview with Alan Hunter, President of the Law Society of Alberta, speaks of the growth of national and international law firms. This process will accelerate under the Free Trade Agreement, pushing law firms towards "advertising, lobbying, and franchising which is a way of life in the United States legal system". Law Societies (and the governing bodies of other professional groups) are no doubt studying the implications of the Agreement upon their respective professions. This subject is further discussed in the "Highlights" section.

IX Investment and Financial Services

Investments

Chapter 16 of the Free Trade Agreement allows for investments by each country within the territory of the other. Investors must be accorded "no less favorable" treatment than that accorded domestic businesses. Investments could include establishing a new business, acquiring an existing business, or the operation, conduct or sale of such businesses (Art. 1602). Provinces, and states, must accord treatment on the same basis as that which they would give to other provinces or states [Art. 1602(4)].

No term or condition can be imposed as to how such companies conduct their business, nor is there any requirement to purchase goods or services from the host country (Art. 1603). Transfer out of the country, of profits, earnings, or proceeds from sale or liquidation, is not prohibited (Art. 1606).

While this is a privilege intended to work both ways, past history shows a far greater acquisition of Canadian companies by Americans than the reverse. In years past, Canada has conducted close reviews of foreign take-overs before granting approval. Until recently, the law, as set out in the federal "Investment Canada Act", provided that Canadian companies with business assets over $5 million could be denied foreign take-over if they were in healthy financial condition. If such businesses were in financial trouble, a foreign take-over might be allowed. This meant that our larger successful businesses were protected from foreign take-overs.

Under the Free Trade Agreement (Annex to 1607.3) Canada will be required to amend the above mentioned Act so that, in regard to American direct take-overs, there will be no review unless the business assets exceed,

-$25 million during the first year period;
-$50 million during the second year;
-$150 million during the third year.

In the case of "indirect" take-overs, these figures are increased to:

-$100 million during the first year;
-$250 million during the second year;
-$500 million during the third year.

This means that under the Free Trade Agreement there will be no control of American take-overs of Canadian companies unless their assets exceed $150 million after 3 years for direct take-overs, or $500 million for indirect take-overs. The previous figure was $5 million. These amounts are so large that anything less than the C.P.R. would be eligible for American take-over. Some critics call it a virtual "sell out" of Canada.

The Free Trade Bill (C-13O) makes all these amendments to our "Investment Canada Act", which is part of Canada's commitment under the Free Trade Agreement.

Financial Services

Chapter 17 deals with financial services, by which is meant services of a financial nature offered by a financial institution. Each country may operate such services within the territory of the other.

In regard to Canadian-controlled banks and financial institutions operating in the United States, the United States agrees to accord to them the same treatment as it accords its own domestic institutions (Art. 1702).

American-controlled banks operating in Canada will be exempt from several provisions of the Canadian Bank Act, which apply to other foreign banks. For example they are not required to limit their Canadian assets to 8% of the total domestic assets of all Canadian banks or seek government _approval before opening additional branches.

Also, American-controlled banks operating in Canada will be permitted to transfer loans to their parent bank. [Art. 1703 (2)(d)]. These concessions to American financial institutions operating in Canada require extensive changes to our Bank Act, and will place them in a favored position over other foreign banks. All the required amendments are included in Bill C-130.

X Canada's Social Programs

Social Programs Are Vulnerable

The Free Trade Agreement makes no direct reference to Canada's extensive health, social, and employee benefit programs. This omission has led many Canadians to assume that Canada's social welfare programs are intact and secure. This assumption, however, overlooks the indirect hazards to which they will be exposed under the Free Trade deal.

The kinds of programs referred to here include the following:

- Canada's universal health and medical care
  system;
- Unemployment Insurance;
- Canada Pension Plan;
- Regional Development Programs and govern
  ment subsidies

The risk is that some of these benefits, long enjoyed by Canadians, but unknown to American workers, could be challenged at some time in the future by the United States as being "unfair subsidies". Pressure to change or eliminate them could come from two sources: both American and Canadian industries.

Pressure From American Industry

As goods move freely between Canada and the United States, some Canadian commodities will enter the United States at a lower price than similar American goods. The United States, in order to protect its own industries, could declare that the government subsidies and regional development programs enjoyed by Canadian industry are "unfair subsidies". The United States could either insist on their removal or impose a countervailing duty equivalent to the value of such benefits (to bring the price to the level of the competing

American product). Thus, Canada's trade with the United States could be penalized because of our regional development and subsidies programs.

In the more distant future, U.S. industry might put pressure on the Canadian government to eliminate those benefits altogether as constituting "unfair trade practices", and as being contrary to one of the stated "objectives" of the Free Trade Agreement which is "to facilitate conditions of fair competition within the Free-Trade area" [Art.102(c)].

Pressure From Canadian Industry

While Canada's social programs, health care, unemployment insurance, and pensions, are designed to benefit workers. However, the employer must also pay a share of the premiums, the cost of which is added to the sale price of the commodity being produced. The time could come when Canadian industry exerts pressure on the Federal Government to eliminate these programs which are costly to employers and reduce their competitiveness in the export trade.

There is a strange anomaly here, as it finds one type of benefit program being attacked by American industry, and another being attacked by Canadian industry, each alleging harmful effects on trade. It demonstrates the uncertain position of Canada's social programs under the Free Trade Agreement. They could become a contentious issue in competitive trading with the United States. The subjects of health care and other social benefits are further discussed in the "Highlights" section.

XI Other Provisions

There are other provisions tucked away in less obvious parts of the Free Trade Agreement which deserve to be mentioned.

Federal-Provincial Relations:

Article 103 - The Federal Government must assure observance of the Agreement by the provinces even though this might infringe on areas of provincial autonomy.

Article. 2104 - The Federal Government can agree on modifications or additions to the Agreement, which in turn would be binding on the provinces. This is a very wide power to be left to federal political leaders and a break from Canadian tradition.

Article. 502 - This is Chapter 5, headed "National Treatment" and consists of only two Articles. It is the shortest Chapter in the Agreement and probably the most difficult to assess in terms of its implications. Paraphrased, it says this: whatever favorable treatment a province of Canada gives to goods received from other parts of Canada must also be given to American states. Similarly, any favorable treatment which an American state gives to similar goods from other states must also be given to Canadian provinces. A logical question is, Are provincial governments aware of this? - they are nonetheless bound by it.

Nullification and Impairment Clause

Article. 2011 forbids either country applying any "measure" (defined in Art. 201 as "any law, regulation, procedure, requirement or practice") which would reduce the benefits that the other country could reasonably expect, directly or indirectly, from the Free Trade Agreement.

There are times when Canadians might invoke this clause against any procedure or practice adopted by the United States that reduces the benefits which Canadians should reasonably expect from the FTA. It could also be used as a bargaining tool for the United States to challenge Canadian practices such as funding for regional development designed to aid less prosperous regions of Canada.

Indeed, the possibility of challenges arising from either side under this Article has led some commentators to view Article 2011 as the real "sleeper" in the Free Trade Agreement.

Monopolies Articles

The term "monopoly" is meant to refer to any plan, scheme, or system for providing a national service, which Americans may see as a monopoly. If, for example, Canada were to introduce a national car insurance scheme to reduce premium costs for Canadians, Article 2010 would require us to give advance notice to the United States, engage in consultations if they so requested, and then be prepared to compensate American private insurance companies which might be adversely affected through loss of business. This is a shocking suggestion, but not altogether unfounded. It all relates to the different attitudes of our countries towards the role of government.

The United States operates on an "open market" system or a policy of non-intervention by government. It is the philosophy of individual initiative, the "survival-of-the-fittist" mentality with the emphasis on competition. By way of contrast, Canada historically has had unique problems which could be addressed only through national initiatives. We have a huge country with a small scattered population and intense regional disparities requiring comprehensive schemes to equalize benefits to all segments of this diverse nation. Americans, on the other hand, do not see this as a function of government. This basic difference in attitude could lead to future misunderstandings as to the intent of Article 2010, and Canada may will find herself defending programs and schemes that historically have been a basic feature of national life. Article 2010 has the potential for philosophical misunderstanding between our two countries in the future.

Government Procurement

This refers to procurement or purchase of "eligible goods" (manufactured or unmanufactured) by government departments in each country. The aim is for liberalization of such government purchases so that each country will have equal opportunities to supply government contracts of the other.

Already GATT is working towards such liberalization on a multi-national basis. What the Free Trade Agreement (Chapter 13) is meant to do is to augment the GATT provisions (Art. 1302-3), and in particular to cover all government supply contracts valued at over $25,000.

The government departments to which this applies, Canadian and American, are listed in the Annex as well as the kinds of goods eligible for coverage. These include the following:

- equipment for railways, engines, power transmission, agriculture, air conditioners;
- fire fighting and rescue equipment; plumbing; heating; sanitation and cleaning; water purification; data processing; medical, dental and veterinarian supplies;
- furniture; office equipment; musical instruments; recreation and athletic equipment; live animals; ores and minerals.

On all of these items each country is to have access to bidding and equal evaluation of the bids submitted. In other words, it is an "open bidding" policy, enabling suppliers from each country to bid on government contracts of the other. This does not apply, however, to contracts set aside for small business (General Note to Annex).

Supplying goods to the Canadian government is a large and lucrative business valued over $70 million annually. With Canada's smaller population there is likely to be a heavier volume of bidding from the United States for Canadian government contracts than the reverse. Because American production costs are lower, we could be entering a bidding contest that is prejudicial to our country. If contracts are awarded to American companies, much of the work could be done in American plants using American labor and materials.

Technical Standards

This pertains to Federal Government approval of a product as having fulfilled certain criteria to permit its use in a specific manner for a specific purpose. Agricultural products are excepted. Neither country, under Free Trade, will be able to enforce standard-related measures (i.e. technical specifications, regulations, standards or rules) that would create an "unnecessary barrier to trade" (Art. 603). In other words, in matters of trade, our government could not refuse approval of a product solely on the ground that certain technical standards had been violated, if the United States regarded such standards as an interference to free trade. Standard-related measures of both countries are to be made "compatible" (Art. 604.).

Suppose Canada, in purchasing machinery from an American factory, objected that in its production certain of our environmental standards had been violated. Such a complaint might be regarded as an "unnecessary barrier to trade". The requirement under Free Trade for conformity in our technical standards may at some point require Canada to compromise its own standards.

It is hard to predict where this would end, with the technical changes and advances likely to occur in the decades ahead. One thing is certain however; Canada will be less free to introduce, maintain, and enforce whatever present or future standards it may choose to adopt.

Dispute Settlement Mechanism

There are two procedures in the Free Trade Agreement for settling disputes. These pertain to:

- Disputes arising in Anti-Dumping and
   Countervailing duty cases (Chapter 19);
- General Disputes (Chapter 18).

A discussion on each follows:

Disputes Arising in Anti-Dumping and Countervailing Duty Cases

As previously mentioned, present laws governing anti-dumping and countervailing duties will continue in effect for five years and if necessary for seven years. During this period new trade rules will be negotiated though existing duties will not necessarily be removed. If no system of rules is agreed upon within this period, either party may terminate the Agreement on six months' notice (Article 1906).

In the event that disputes arise concerning these duties during the negotiating period, the Agreement sets out a procedure for their settlement (Chapter 19). The mechanism for such dispute resolution is as follows:

- Where either country objects to a duty imposed by the other country, it can appeal to a "binational panel" consisting of five members jointly chosen by both countries:
- The panel conducts a review and makes a recommendation, but in doing so it applies the law of the country which has imposed the duty (Art. 1904.3). In other words, if the United

States has levied a countervailing duty on goods from Canada, the panel will simply decide if such duty complies with American law. It will be overturned only if the United States is breaking its own trade law.
- The decision of the panel is binding and there is no appeal. Article 1904.11 states:

> Neither party shall provide in its domestic legislation for an appeal from a panel decision to a domestic court.

This means, it is an administrative decision not subject to judicial review.
- Article 1904.9 says the decision of the panel is "binding" on the parties. Yet there is no provision for enforcement if a country fails to honour the panel decision. All that the aggrieved country can do is impose similar duties on the other country in retaliation or terminate the Free Trade Agreement on sixty days' notice [Article 1903.3(b)].

A press release date-lined Washington D.C. July 2, 1988 reported that American officials were disturbed as to how panel decisions would be implemented. As a result of subsequent discussions in the U.S. Trade Representative's office, a spokesman stated "We expect everything to fall into place now". It is hard to decipher what such a statement means. Suffice to say that the written words of the Agreement (which will be the ultimate test in any dispute) say nothing about enforcement of panel decisions other than retaliation or termination. This can only be regarded as a serious deficiency.

Canada is likely to be at a particular disadvantage when it comes to negotiations over new trade laws and rules about subsidies as many Canadian industries rely on government subsidies to help them survive. An article in the New York Times (June 5, 1988) stated:

Canada spends 2.3% of its Gross Domestic Product on subsidies, compared with 0.4% of the gross national product in the United States.

It is clear that if subsidies are reduced or removed as a result of these negotiations, Canada will be more adversely affected than the United States. Actually, the FTA leaves one of the stickiest issues to be worked out after the pact comes into effect.

General Dispute-Settlement Mechanism

This is the long-range permanent mechanism for settling major disputes for as long as the Free Trade Agreement is in existence. The procedure is described in Chapter 18. The kind of disputes dealt with here are very broad, namely:

(a) Interpretation of the Free Trade Agreement and its application;
(b) Complaints by either country about measures by the other which are considered inconsistent with the Agreement;
(c) Complaints under Article 2011. This is called the "Nullification and Impairment" clause. Where challenges arise, the aggrieved country may invoke certain of the remedial procedures in Chapter 18.

In regard to disputes of a general nature as described above,the procedure for dispute resolution is as follows,

1. The first stage is to try to reach a solution through "consultation" (Art. 1804).
2. If this is not successful within thirty days, either party can request a hearing before the "Canada-U.S. Trade Commission". This Commission has top-level representatives from

both countries, but it does its work through committees, working groups, and panels.

3. If the Commission does not resolve the matter within thirty days, and if it is not an emergency, the Commission will refer it to "binding arbitration".

4. Arbitration is conducted by a panel of at least two representatives from each country, plus a Chairman, all drawn from a roster of names submitted by both countries (Art. 1807).

5. The Arbitration Panel decides on its own procedure. Its initial report must be made within three months. Both parties are given an opportunity to comment on the preliminary findings, and present written objections, before the panel completes its final report.

6. The final report of the Arbitration Panel goes back to the Commission, which then prepares a "resolution" usually conforming with the panel's findings (Art. 1807).

7. If a country fails to implement the findings of the Arbitrator, the other country "may suspend equivalent benefits" to the non-complying country, that is, retaliate (Art. 1807.9).

8. There is no reference to any appeal, and more significantly, no procedure for enforcing compliance with the ruling of the Arbitrator or of the resolution of the Commission.

Canadians have been led to believe that the Free Trade Agreement provides a binding mechanism for the resolution of disputes. If by "binding" we mean the right to "retaliate" then this may be so. To be binding in law, however, remedies or sanctions are required to redress breaches, and assure compliance. By no reasonable interpretation does the Free Trade Agreement provide this. Without binding mechanism for settlement of disputes, any agreement is rendered impotent. The only option available to the parties is a trade war.

A similar conclusion is noted in the Wall Street

Journal even though it is known to be a proponent of the trade deal. An editorial in the issue of June 13, 1988, in which it analyzed deficiencies in the enforcement of panel decisions, it concluded with these words: "If American violators can't be punished, the trade agreement will be dead" (Press report June 15, 1988). Canadians should seriously ponder this deficiency in the Free Trade Agreement.

Provinces should also be reminded that they have no standing before the Commission; yet any number of provincial measures could be subject to challenge. If this happens, all of the above procedures will be followed, but the Province affected will not be there. Instead, it would be represented by federally-appointed commissioners, panelists and arbitrators.[1]

The Six-Month Termination Clause

As indicated above, either country can terminate the Agreement for any of the following reasons:

(1) If negotiations for new trade laws (defining unfair subsidies and countervailing duties) are not finalized in seven years (Art. 1906);
(2) If during that five-to seven-year-period, differences have arisen over present duties, and one country has failed to comply with the ruling of the bi-national panel (Art. 1903);
(3) Even, it seems, without any apparent reason. Chapter 21 provides that the Agreement shall remain in force unless terminated by either party on six months' notice.

Some Canadians have been heard to say, "Let's sign the Agreement anyway. We can terminate it on six months' notice if we don't like it".

However, it is definitely not so simple. For one

---

[1] See articles in January 1988 issue of "National Canadian Bar Association" publication - p. 12 et seq.

thing, the termination clause works both ways. The United States could use it against Canada to force agreement on certain concessions by threatening to pull out - at a time unsuitable to Canada. This could arise, in the controversial subject of unfair subsidies and countervailing duties which must still be worked out during the coming years. The United States might threaten to terminate the Agreement unless the new definitions are to their satisfaction.

No matter which country were to terminate the Agreement, it could place Canada in a serious predicament. Once the Agreement takes effect in January 1989, Canadian industries would begin 'gearing up' in anticipation of greater exports to the United States. This could include costly capital expenditures for upgrading factories, modernizing equipment, and re-training workers. Once Canada had embarked on an industrial conversion process, cancellation would create another major disruption to our national economy. Indeed we would be in a worse position if we were to enter into the Agreement, then terminate it, than if we had never entered into it at all.

For these reasons, termination cannot be looked upon as a "way out". It is better that Canadians understand the Agreement now, before giving it final approval.

XII Implementation of Free Trade

Hasty Approval of Free Trade

Both Canada, and the United States, must pass enabling legislation before the end of 1988, or the Free Trade Agreement will die. Recently the United States has indicated its willingness to extend the date, indicating how anxious they are to obtain Canada's approval.

On May 24, 1988, the Federal Government tabled Bill C-130 in the House of Commons, entitled "Canada-United States Free Trade Agreement Implementation Act". It was strongly opposed by both Opposition parties (Liberals and New Democrats) who took the position that it was a sell-out of Canadian sovereignty. The New Democrat Party House Leader, Nelson Riis, contended that the Bill was too large to be considered as a single unit, and that it should be divided into a series of Bills. The Speaker rejected that motion on June 8.

On second reading the Tories imposed a five day limit on debate and then invoked closure, after which the Bill was referred to a committee of sixteen (twelve of whom were from the Party in power). No cross-country hearings were held; persons wishing to make presentations were required to travel to Ottawa and were restricted as to time. When the Bill returned to the House of Commons for final reading, the Tories imposed a four-day limit on debate, followed by closure. The Bill passed third reading in the House of Commons on August 31, 1988, by a vote of 177 to 64, and then proceeded to the Senate where it awaits final approval.

It is the concern of many that this Bill, which is perhaps one of the most important ever to come before the Canadian Parliament, is proceeding to its possible final passage almost un-read and un-examined.

Bill C-130, *The Free Trade Agreement Implementation Act*

An indication of the magnitude of this Bill is its length. It contains 123 pages. It makes sweeping amendments to 27 existing federal statutes, and will have an indirect bearing on several pieces of provincial legislation. The five words in Section 7: "The Agreement is hereby approved" will bring into effect the monumental Free Trade Agreement, discussed in the preceding pages.

The list of federal Acts being amended is formidable. It is enlightening to examine them. They are:

-Special Import Measures Act
-Federal Court Act
-Agricultural Products Standards Act
-Department of Agriculture Act
-Bank Act
-Broadcasting Act
-Canadian Wheat Board Act
-Copyright Act
-Customs Act
-Excise Tax Act
-Export and Import Permits Act
-Canada Grain Act
-Importation of Grain Act
-Importation of Intoxicating Liquors Act
-Income Tax Act
-Canadian and British Insurance Companies Act
-Investment-Canada Act
-Investment Companies Act
-Loan Companies Act
-Meat Import Act
-Meat Inspection Act
-National Energy Board Act
-Seeds Act
-Standard Council of Canada Act
-Statistics Act
-Textile and Clothing Act

-Trust Companies Act
-Western Grain Transportation Act

A perusal of this list gives an idea of the extent to which implementation of the Free Trade Agreement will fundamentally change Canadian statute law. Bill C-130 makes it possible for the Federal Government to encroach on provincial powers. For example, Ottawa must ensure observance of the Free Trade Agreement by provincial and local governments (Article 103). The same applies to any future amendments and additions which may be made to the Agreement (Article 2104). Bill C-130 (section 6) goes even further by providing that:

> ...for greater certainty...nothing in this Act....limits in any manner the right of Parliament to enact legislation to implement any provision of the Agreement or fulfil any of the obligations of the Government of Canada under the Agreement.

It is this Bill which has passed the House of Commons and is now before the Senate.

The Response of The Provinces

The response from various provinces has been as follows:

1. Alberta, Saskatchewan and Quebec gave immediate endorsement to the Free Trade Agreement.
2. Manitoba: The current political situation in Manitoba, a minority government, will make it difficult for the government to endorse the Free Trade Agreement in the light of objections expressed by both opposition parties.
3. Prince Edward Island: Premier Ghiz is an adamant opponent of the Free Trade Agreement.

His public speeches show a comprehensive grasp of the implications of the deal, regarding not only his own province's fishing and farming industries, but also Canada's sovereign rights as a nation. Instead of the promised access to the American market, he says the Agreement subjects Canada to American trade laws. Speaking of President Reagan's "level playing field", Premier Ghiz says:

> The Americans have shown a disturbing tendency to create a level playing field with a distinct tilt in their favor by simply defining whatever anybody else does as an unfair subsidy, and what they do as right and just and proper.

4. Ontario has been a vocal opponent. Premier Peterson has expressed several areas of concern about the Free Trade Agreement and Bill C-130, among them the following:

> (a) The "wine and spirits" provision prohibiting mark-ups on American wine and liquor which have long been in effect to protect Ontario grape-growers and the infant wine industry;
> (b) In its export of electricity to the United Stated, Ontario takes the position that it has the right to charge more for electricity sold to the United States than that to domestic consumers. Second, that it has the right to export only what is surplus to Canada's needs. Both of these are contrary to Article 904 should shortages arise;
> (c) Ontario's new Health Care Bill, introduced into the Legislature in June 1988, allowing private health care clinics to operate in the province, specifies that

preference is to be given to Canadian-operated clinics over American-operated ones. This is contrary to the Free Trade Agreement provisions on investment and services (Press report June 4, 1988).

Other statements of Premier Peterson are:

a) That the federal Bill infringes on provincial powers;
b) That the Federal Government has no right to implement areas of foreign treaties that fall within provincial jurisdiction;
c) That Ontario refuses to comply with "a deal that makes too many concessions to Washington for too few benefits".

Ontario's position has exposed a strange inconsistency between Bill C-13O and the Meech Lake Accord. Bill C-13O is a strong assertion of federal power. Yet under the Meech Lake Accord, the Federal Government willingly transferred many of its powers to the provinces. This enhanced stature of the provinces is something which Ontario seems to have chosen to exercise.

XIII Summary and Conclusions

General

1. The writer favors freer trade, but not this Free Trade Agreement. The cost of securing the remaining 20% of our trade with the United States is unreasonable and excessive.
2. With the apparent decline of the United States as the world economic leader, and the rise of Asian-Pacific countries as the future zone of expanding world trade, a better option for Canada is to develop multi-national trade relationships, especially with countries in the Pacific
3. Countervailing duties, which are the greatest barrier to Free Trade, will not be eliminated by the Agreement.

What Canadians Will Gain

1. Consumer goods imported from the United States will be cheaper initially. However they will be cheaper still from Hong Kong, Korea, China, and Japan.
2. Jobs in some industries may increase, such as oil and gas, though only in these industries if OPEC prices rise. Export profits relate less to market access than to pricing, which under the Free Trade Agreement will be governed by factors beyond Canadian control. The Federal Government's own prediction is that the Canadian economy will create more new jobs in the next ten years than will Free Trade. The loss of jobs through the exodus of business and industry will be substantial.
3. Canadian "big business" will profit through expansion to American markets, provided such companies survive competition from cheaper American products, possible take-over, and closure.

1. Oil and Gas - Article 904

When shortages are declared Canada must export to the United States a fixed proportion of its total energy supply at a price no higher than its domestic price. In agreeing with this Canada has thus given away its control over supplies and pricing, and any hope of national energy self-sufficiency.

2. Control over natural resources, (minerals such as zinc, copper and aluminum), (Article 409).

Canada must sell to the United States a fixed proportion of its total export shipments of these commodities in times of shortage at a price no higher than that charged domestically. This loss of control over supply and pricing of our natural resources when these become scare means that Canadians will have no priority over Americans in the use of our nation's resources.

3. Agriculture - Chapter 7

This Part of the Free Trade Agreement is so massive and complex that even agricultural economists have difficulty assessing its effect. Its provisions are nonetheless analyzed for agriculturalists to evaluate.

4 Wine and Spirits - Article 803

Curtailing mark-ups on American wine and spirits could eventually destroy Canada's wine industry.

5. Services - Chapter 14

American-controlled enterprises operating in Canada may bring in their own service personnel [Articles 1402(7), 1403, 1405]. This would remove job opportunities otherwise available to Canadians, especially in positions traditionally held by women.

6. Temporary Entry - Chapter 15

American enterprises engaged in Free Trade activities in Canada can bring in their own technical workers and professionals. There is no time limit on how long they can stay; only that they have no intention of establishing a permanent residence. This could go on for as long as the free-trade enterprise continued, be it the construction of a hydro-power dam, or the operation of a health care clinic. Canadians would not have normal access to such jobs, and some workers could be replaced.

7. Investment - Chapter 16

The door is open to American corporate take-overs of Canadian businesses (Article 1602) - with no terms or conditions imposed as to their operation (Article 1603). This is what Opposition parties call "the sell-out" of Canada.

8. Financial Services - Chapter 17

American-controlled banks operating in Canada will have special privileges not enjoyed by other foreign banks, namely:

a) Assets not limited to 8% of total assets of all Canadian banks;
b) Ministerial approval not required for opening of new branches.

9. Government Procurement - Chapter 13

The huge contracts for suppling the Federal Government will no longer be limited to Canadian bidders. These will now be open to bidding from American competitors. These contracts have been a lucrative source of income for Canadian suppliers and employees.

10. Technical Standards - Chapter 6

Canadian technical standards are to be made "compatible" with those of the United States. This could mean that Canada will have to compromise on some of its standards, even in the environmental field.

11. Canada's Social Programs

The omission of these from the Free Trade Agreement does not mean they are secure. Some could be vulnerable to attack as "unfair subsidies" and be subject to countervailing duties, or to pressure for their reduction or elimination. Canada has extensive social benefit programs which do not exist on the same scale in the United States. These are: Canada's health care system, Unemployment Insurance benefits, the Canada Pension Plan, Old Age Security, Family Allowance, Equalization Payments to poor provinces, subsidies to

industries, Regional Development programs, and could eventually include federally-funded day-care. Possible challenges to these programs are discussed further under the heading "Health Care" in the "Highlights" section.
12. Water

Water is not covered in the Free Trade Agreement. It is not enough to rely on political promises that Canada will not be forced to export water to the United States. Once the Free Trade Agreement comes into effect, Canada will be in a poor bargaining position against American pressure to divert water if there is no legislation to forbid it. Canada's proposed "Water Preservation Act" died with the dissolution of parliament on October 1, 1988. Pressure has already been exerted for diverting water from the Great Lakes into the drought-stricken Mississippi basin. In the on-going bargaining implicit in the Free Trade Agreement, Canada throughout will be the weaker party at the negotiating table. Our lack of success on the acid rain issue is indicative of that.

Dispute Resolution

The Free Trade Agreement does not provide legally-binding mechanisms for the resolution of disputes. Despite elaborate provision for panels and arbitrators, it contains no sanctions to redress breaches, or assure compliance with panel decisions, except by retaliation or termination. Without adequate enforcement, any agreement is rendered deficient and ineffective.

Six Month Termination Clause

This is not the "easy way out" that some people imagine. It works both ways and could backfire on Canada. It could be used as a weapon by the United States to enforce its future demands by threatening to pull out, perhaps at a time unsuitable to Canada. Once the Agreement is in effect, and Canadian industry 'gears up' to anticipated greater exports, termination could create a disruption to the Canadian economy. It has been said that Canada has never pulled out of an agreement with the United States. If it were to do so on this, the most monumental of all, American retaliation could be horrendous in terms of trade relations. It is better for Canadians to understand the Agreement before giving it endorsement.

Sovereignty

Under the Free Trade Agreement, ownership and control of Canadian industry and resources will gravitate to the United States. With that, decision-making will be transferred to the board rooms of New York and Washington.

Political power is known to eventually follow the movement of economic power. It is not improbable that Canada could face the eventual loss of political independence, and of its sovereignty as a nation.

Conclusions

In conclusion the writer would emphasize that most, though not all, of the provisions noted above are reciprocal. However, the purpose here has been to analyze the effects upon Canada.

Some Canadians will benefit from the freedom to move into the American work force and into American industry. But the over-riding factor in all such movement, is the economic inequality between Canada and the United States.

What Canada has given away to clear the remaining 20% of our trade is enormous. The most serious is our potential loss of control over our oil, gas and natural resources, both in respect to supply and price.

We have given unfettered freedom to American banks operating in Canada and to foreign take-overs of Canadian industries and services. We have given American workers and professionals engaged in any "Free Trade enterprise or activity" freedom to enter

Canada temporarily. We have escalated the threat to all our social benefit programs, government subsidies, and regional development programs. As one observer said on completion of the Free Trade negotiations, "Canada has certainly been 'out-hustled' on this one".

There can be no equality where one partner is the most powerful nation on earth, the other a subordinate on the world stage: where one has a population of 260 million, the other only 26 million. Unlike the European Economic Community which is a union of twelve relatively equal nations, this is an unequal union, reminiscent of a walrus and a frog or an elephant and a mouse. Such a union can have only one result; the smaller being swallowed by the larger.

Bill C-13O, which is to implement the Free Trade Agreement in Canada, contains sweeping revisions of existing Canadian statute law, on a scale unprecedented in a single Act. It also encroaches on provincial powers.

In the little time that remains Canadians can ponder not so much what the Free Trade Agreement will do to certain segments of our economy, but rather what it will do to Canada as a whole - now and in the future.

Editor's Note:
The following section is a collection of highlights
of major concerns compiled by the author.

XIV Highlights of Major Concerns
From The Canadian Perspective

The Agreement is not what it seems

The Free Trade Agreement Does Not Insure "Free Trade"
Because-

>-Countervailing duties, the chief barrier to Free Trade, remain to be resolved after the Agreement takes effect.
>-The American Omnibus Trade Bill, of 1988, did not exempt Canada from harsh new American protectionist laws, despite assurances to the contrary throughout the trade negotiations.

Its Not Just a Trade Agreement

Because-
>-It includes many chapters unrelated to trade.

Services

This is the most comprehensive trade in services agreement ever negotiated between two countries.
The 299 categories of services listed by code number only include:

>a) Workers in such industries as: agriculture; forestry; construction; and mining.
>b) Persons engaged in real estate; insurance; wholesale distribution; tourism; restaurant and clerical services, computer and telecommunications.
>c) Management services for: retail businesses; hospitals of all kinds; public health clinics; home care; ambulance services; and office management services for physicians and dentists.

d) Commercial operation of blood banks and medical laboratories.

The significance of the service industry to Canada is as follows:

a) 10 million Canadians are employed in this field representing 70% of Canada's labour force.
b) The greatest number of new jobs in Canada in the past ten years have been in the service sector of the economy.
c) 83% of employed women work in these fields.

The Free Trade Agreement grants special concessions to U.S. service industries:

a) There is no need to establish a commercial presence in Canada (1402.8). This is particularly relevant to the telecommunications industry
b) Personnel are to be accorded "national treatment", (Article 105); that is the same treatment accorded Canadian citizens.

Federal Government Reports

a) The MacDonald Commission, commonly cited as the prime advocate of Free Trade, had little to say about services in its three-volume report. Out of its seventy-two background papers, none dealt with trade in services.
b) The Clyne Commission, 1979 which investigated international trade in telecommunications stated that American provision of such services would be a dangerous threat to Canadian sovereignty.

The practical effect on Canada of trade in services means:

a) More American employees will be brought into Canada to work in American-controlled businesses;
b) Multi-nationals will be under no obligation to hire Canadians;

Some service industries will be centralized in the United States, such as telecommunications resulting in job losses for Canadians.

Two questions have been raised:

First, would Americans working in Canada be required to pay Canada employee benefit premiums? - If not, would that be an incentive to hire them in place of Canadian workers?

Second, if a recession occurs in the United States, could American multi-nationals save the jobs of their American employees by moving them to their Canadian business enterprises?

Temporary Entry of Business Persons

The categories covered are extensive:

persons engaged in sales; marketing and distribution; management and supervisory personnel; computer specialists; insurers; bankers; investment brokers; public relations persons; advertising and tourism personnel.

It also includes 45 classes of professions (Schedule 2, Annex 1502.1), amongst them:

accountants; engineers; scientists (14 categories); teaching and research medical personnel; architects; dentists; nurses; psychologists; lawyers; teachers (collage level); economists;

social workers; counsellors; hotel managers; librarians, dieticians; management consultants; and many others.

The argument is heard that Canadians are equally competent to compete in any of these fields. The issue is not one of competence, but of population imbalance (26 million as opposed to 260 million). Canadians entering the United States, even in substantial numbers, would be only a trickle compared to the total number of Americans in any particular category. Conversely, a small number of Americans entering Canada would constitute a flood, which could easily dominate the categories affected.

American Investment In Canada

Restrictions are to be virtually eliminated with a review only where assets exceed $150 million.
Some comparative figures:

-Canadian investment in the United States increased from $20 billion in 1980 to $45 billion in 1987.

-American investment in Canada increased from $50 billion in 1980 to $75 billion in 1987.

-U.S. investment in Canada represents a far greater percentage of ownership in the Canadian economy than does Canadian investment in the United States.

-The American economy is twelve times that of Canada and can more readily absorb foreign investment without a significant impact on its economic base.

-Canada's smaller economy cannot absorb the magnitude of U.S. investment without serious distortion of its economic balance.

Removal of tariffs may mean some companies operating in Canada will move to the United States. Canadian jobs will be lost. Examples are:

> -American branch plants operating in Canada;
> -American-owned business in Canada may choose to supply the Canadian market from an American location where population is greater, markets larger, and operating costs less.
> -Increased take-overs of successful Canadian operations could result in closure and removal to new American headquarters.
> -New businesses considering starting up in Canada may find it more advantageous to locate in the United States instead.

Loss of jobs and potential jobs for Canadians will be the result of this Free Trade Agreement.

Open Bidding On Government Supply Contracts

The Canadian economy is too small for Canadian suppliers to successfully out-bid their American counterparts on either Canadian or American government contracts. This has been a multi-million-dollar business for Canadians, involving some thirty government departments and vast range of products, materials, and services.

The previous Canadian policy was to purchase supplies outside Canada only when they were not available here. Loss of these contracts will have a serious effect on Canadian businesses and employment. It has little to do with Free Trade and represents another step towards commercial union with the United Stated.

Energy

Because of conflicting interpretations of the energy provisions in the Free Trade Agreement, the following is presented as an additional commentary.

The key provisions here are mandatory proportionate sharing of supplies with the United States and an export price not exceeding the domestic price.

These provisions apply both to energy (Art.904) and to natural resources (Art.409), These articles being almost identical.

It will be seen that the above articles deal with two requirements: pricing and supply.

As to pricing, Article 903 already forbids levying"any tax, duty or charge" on exports at any time unless these apply to domestic sales as well. This is true whether Article 904 is in effect or not. If Article 904 is activated in the manner described, then we could not differentiate between what we charge the United States and what we charge domestically.

The second requirement is for proportionate sharing of supplies. The question here, as with pricing, is when the requirement comes into play.

The preamble to Article 904 refers to two Articles in the GATT (to which both our countries belong). Both these articles, XI and XX deal with supplies. They say that we can introduce restrictions, or cut-backs on production, provided we comply with those two articles. The first [Article XI:2(a)] says we can restrict exports if there is a critical shortage. The second (Article XX) says we can cut back production for other reasons as well. Until now, if we wanted to restrict exports, we were free to do so under either of these GATT Articles, and for any of those reasons.

Now under the Free Trade Agreement, if we want to take those same steps and cut back on production, the proportionate sharing provision of Article 904 will come into play. This means we will now be committed to provide the United States with a proportionate share of our remaining supplies. This we were not committed to do before the Free Trade Agreement. When this Article comes into effect, we will have to export to the United States, a proportion equal to that supplied during the previous three years, and we must not disrupt "normal channels of supply" [(904)(c)].

The Federal Government seems to take the position that all we need to do is to avoid declaring a critical shortage under Article XI of GATT, and then Article 904 would not apply. This ignores the fact, however, that Article 904 can be activated for reasons other than critical shortage, that is for reasons mentioned in Article XX of GATT. These reasons include domestic requirements or the need for conservation. The Federal Government indicates that all we need to do is to cancel the licences of multi-national oil companies.

If that interpretation were correct, then we could well ask why Article 904 was included at all, if it could be vitiated so easily. It must have been put there for a purpose, of which the Americans are well aware, namely that whenever Canada cuts back on production, for whatever reason, Americans will be entitled to a proportionate share of whatever is left.

What happens when Article 904 comes into effect is this: if the cut-back in production is to 80% of capacity, then the United States will be entitled to 40% (which happens to be their current share) of the remaining 80%. Mathematically, this represents a greater cut-back for Canada than the United States.

This is the effect of Articles 904 (in respect to energy) and of 409 (respecting natural resources). There is no way to avoid compliance, once Canada, for whatever reason, curtails production.

In calculating the U.S. share of Canadian oil, a report of the Federal Energy Department ("The Canadian Oil Market") indicated that during the quarter ending June 30, 1988, the United States substantially increased its imports of Canadian oil; while at the same time, it substantially reduced its oil exports into Canada. These are the present figures: the United States buys 40% of all crude oil produced in Canada; but Canada receives only 3% of its oil from the United States (mostly for

On Guard For Thee

eastern Canada). It would appear that the United States is "positioning" itself so that when the time comes to determine the proportionate share to which the United States is entitled, that proportion will be substantial.

Reference is frequently made to Quebec Hydro which is selling power to the United States at a price above that charged to domestic consumers. There is no question that this practice will become vulnerable to challenge once the Free Trade Agreement comes into force; as well as Quebec policy of giving preference to Quebec suppliers in the purchase of items such as engines and equipment.

The United States may choose not to invoke this challenge, though it would have the right to do so, due to their great need for Canadian hydro at any price. Choosing not to do so, however, does not mean that such practices are compatible with the Free Trade Agreement.

Canada's Social Programs

Canada has a wide variety of social programs such as Old Age Security, Family Allowance, and the Canada Pension Plan. These could eventually become lost in the "harmonization" process inherent in the Free Trade Agreement. By this we mean the emphasis on the blending of our two systems to insure greater equality in trade.

Programs which will be particularly vulnerable are those linked with the production of goods, that is unemployment insurance, regional development, and government subsidies to industry. Goods exported from Canada which benefit from such programs could be subject to countervailing duties on the basis of "unfair subsidies". The definition of "unfair subsidies" depends entirely on the application of American trade laws.

Some illustrations follow:

a) Unemployment Insurance: This was raised by the United States in the Maritime's ground-fish case, along with about 50 challenges to other programs, some of which were upheld and countervailing duties imposed. The challenge to unemployment insurance was dismissed, but it could be raised again, even successfully.

b) Regional Development Programs: These are designed to help areas of Canada which are economically depressed. There is no comparable regional assistance in the United States other than for areas which accept a military facility. There are already indications that Canada's programs will be considered an "unfair subsidy" and challenged under the Free Trade Agreement.

c) Government Subsidies To Industry: Many Canadian industries have benefited from government subsidies: the textile industry in Ontario; fisheries in the Maritimes; wine producers in British Columbia and mines in the Yukon. It would be a serious blow to the Canadian economy if these were removed. Few of these industries would survive without government assistance. However, They are extremely vulnerable to challenge, especially if the resulting products compete with American goods.

Canada's Health Care System

Of all the benefits enjoyed by Canadians, health care is probably the most precious. Little wonder, as Canada has one of the most comprehensive health care systems in the world. By comparison universal access to health care in the United States is non-existent. In the United States Medicare is available to persons over 65 and Medicaid for the poor (requiring a means test). For the vast majority of Americans, the choices are between expensive private health insurance (which 35 million

Americas cannot afford); paying their own medical expenses, or doing without medical care.

It has been said that Canada's program of health care is "a triumph of astute social planning and considerable will". They are both important. It is, however, very costly, absorbing 8.6% of the gross national product. The less efficient American health care system, costs more: 10.6% per capita of the Gross National Product and still leaves millions without public or private coverage.

The Cost Factor

Health care is paid out of the treasury of the Federal Government. It in turn depends on taxation and the principle contributors to that are corporations. A declared goal of the Free Trade Agreement is to increase competition. Canadian industry will be eager to compete and make profits which in turn require reduced operating costs. This will bring demands for cut-backs in government expenditures such as health care which requires a high level of corporate taxation to maintain.

This is where the political will of successive Canadian governments will be tested in the face of demands from corporate leaders whose powers have been enhanced by the Free Trade Agreement

Harmonization

The concept of "harmonization" pervades the whole of the Free Trade Agreement. It is what President Reagan has called "the level playing field". The disparities between our two countries, especially in health care and social benefits, are so vast that one or the other country must change if harmonization is to be achieved. There is little likelihood of such change from the American side.

The United States Implementation Bill which has passed Congress contains nothing to indicate any intention on the part of the United States to make any changes in policy or practice as a result of the Free Trade Agreement.

Much of the so-called "harmonization" will be in the corporate field, with business practices conforming to the American model. In health care, harmonization will mean a shift to "market orientation". Instead of facilities and services being operated by the government, some will be taken over by private firms as in the United States.

Chapter 14 of the Free Trade Agreement on "Services" will open the door to management by private American chains for all types of hospitals (general; extended care; pediatric; rehabilitation; psychiatric and special); and to management of non-institutional health services (public health clinics; home care and ambulance services); and to commercial operation of blood banks at medical laboratories.

The objection of such facilities and services will be to operate for a profit. This can only be achieved by reducing staff, lowering wages, and compromising on standards of patient care. While the trend towards privatization may have already begun in Canada, the effect of the Free Trade Agreement is to speed the process.

Is Health Care An Unfair Subsidy?

So far, American trade law does not classify health care as an unfair subsidy. However, the definition of subsidies is undergoing constant revision by American officials. American legislation implementing the Free Trade Agreement will allow the United States government to monitor, on a continuing basis, all of Canada's subsidy programs in search of unfair subsidies. No other country is subject to such scrutiny. It is unlikely that Canada's health care system will escape close review. It is equally unlikely that the United States will elevate its system to the level of that in Canada. The persistent but unsuccessful efforts of Senator Edward

Kennedy to improve the American health care system proves that.

Some of the issues involving Canada's social programs and health care may be debatable. However, Canadians have reason to be apprehensive about the continuation of these important programs under the Free Trade Agreement.

Summary

The Free Trade Agreement serves the leaders of big business. They were its motivators, and will be its chief beneficiaries.

No one would object to freer trade in goods, especially with the country which is already our freest trading partner. Rather, it is what got appended in the process to which we object.

Canadian negotiators, in what could be regarded could as extremely naive, gave away control over vast areas of our national life. Even more shocking, it was unnecessary. Perhaps this represents priorities other than those of the average Canadian.

None of us knows where the machinery that has been put in motion will lead. Will it be the abundant prosperity that has been promised? Or, as this writer believes, will it be a twentieth century reincarnation of the giant and the dwarf?

What Canada Should Do?

Canada should not succumb to threats of retaliation if we do not approve of the Free Trade Agreement by a specific date. If pressure tactics are to be part of future negotiations under the Agreement, Canadians should indeed be wary.

If it is a good deal, it will still be a good deal a year from now--or whatever time is needed for meaningful reflection by the Canadian people.

Yes, Canada Has A Choice

Some preferred alternatives are these:

1. Strengthen trade links with countries beyond the United States, especially with the growing markets of Asian-Pacific countries. Europe and nations of the Third World;

2. Negotiate sector-by-sector trade agreements with respect to specific industries and products (similar to Auto Pact) rather than a comprehensive sweeping Agreement which places Canada at a disadvantage.

Because of its importance, it would have been preferable to have the Free Trade issue determined by a referendum A matter as important as national sovereignty should not be submerged in a national election.

Editor's Note:

The following section includes the official response of the government which was printed in newspapers across the country and the author's reply. The Government's response is reproduced at the both the author's, and the Government of Canada's request. As well, the Mr. Crosbie's office sent two articles to us asking that they be printed. They are: "Bowker's Medicare-is-doomed Thesis On Free Trade Non sense" and "Lion Of The Day Lacks Credibility". We were told by them that they were the best on the subject. Those two articles and the public response to the second one are included in the "Media Responses" section. We are satisfied that the Government's point of view has been presented.

XV Trade Deal Analysis Flawed - Crosbie

Marjorie Bowker has managed (Control key trade issue, Viewpoint, Aug.17; Free Trade dangerous, says ex-judge, Journal, Sept.2) to get a great deal of her analysis of the Free Trade agreement (FTA) factually wrong.

In a number of instances, clauses have been incorrectly paraphrased or quoted without explanatory language. Far from broadening understanding, the result is a major distortion of the terms of the agreement, particularly its provisions regarding energy, resources, temporary workers, financial services and investment.

Bowker's conclusions regarding job creation and sovereignty are, by her own account, subjective and not supported by analysis; I will therefore confine my rebuttal to point of fact

Bowker is particularly concerned about the energy provisions of the agreement, which she has completely misunderstood. Among a number of incorrect statements, she states that (a), there can be no reduction in the proportion of Canadian supply of oil and gas going to the United States, (b), the price we charge the United States for our oil and gas cannot be higher than than the price charged to Canadian consumers, (c), the only justification for restricting oil and gas exports would be on national security grounds, and (d), U.S. producers could insist that the American government impose a countervailing duty on Canadian oil producers enjoying "unfair subsidies".

Let me deal with these in turn. With regard to allegation (a), Canadians are under absolutely no obligation to sell energy resources, or any other product for that matter, to the U.S, or to provide any specific level of supply. The requirement to provide "access" to a defined proportion of supply applies only in very limited circumstances where a government imposes export restrictions for reasons of conservation, short supply or domestic price stabilization. In these special and unusual circumstances we are obliged only to allow

U.S. companies to bid, in competition with Canadians, up to their historic share. Whether the U.S. buyer gets the contract even in these circumstances will be up to the market place.

Contrary to what Bowker states in her allegation (b), nothing in th FTA prevents Canadian producers of energy from negotiating export prices that are higher than domestic prices. That is why U.S. consumers of Quebec power in New York State will be paying approximately double the rate paid by Quebecers.

Bowker's statements about national security restrictions, allegation (c),are equally off-base. The United States has, from time to time, stopped Canadian exports of uranium for so-called national security reasons; the purpose of the national security article cited by Bowker is to define more precisely and narrowly when they would be entitled to do so. This provision benefits Canada much more that it does the U.S, and was included at our insistence; moreover, it does not prevent the two countries from restricting exports on a number of other grounds, including short supply, conservation and environmental.

Bowker's analysis of subsidies in the oil industry, point (d), is wrong because she has ignored the existence of Article 906 which says that both parties have agreed to allow existing or future incentives for oil and gas exploration, development and related activities. Indeed, a senior U.S. official, reacting to the announcement on Sept.2 of Canadian government support for Huskey Oil Ltd. to produce heavy oil in Saskatchewan and Alberta, was quoted as saying, "I don't think what the Canadian government did in the Huskey deal is inconsistent with the Free Trade agreement at all."

Other errors, on the analysis of SERVICES (contrary to what Bowker says, the agreement will not allow U.S.-controlled health-care facilities to be established in Canada where owners could bring in their own personnel to replace Canadians); TEMPORARY ENTRY (U.S. workers will not be brought in to perform a multitude of services, and have the right to equal treatment with Canadian workers); INVESTMENT (the investment chapter does not mean that anything less than CP (Canadian Pacific) would be eligible for U.S. takeover); FINANCIAL SERVICES (U.S. banks in Canada will not be favored over domestic banks); TECHNICAL STANDARDS (Free Trade will not require Canada to compromise its own standards); dispute settlement (panel decisions in anti-dumping and countervailing duty cases are legally binding on both parties), and in other areas.

I agree that Canadians should have the facts in order to form their own assessments of the value of this trade agreement. They are not served well by Bowker's attempt. For those who want the facts explained in layman's language, there is a variety of publications available in English by phoning 1-800-387-0660, or 1-800-387-0679 if the material is preferred in French. Better still, discuss the issue with someone whose livelihood depends on exports to the United States

XVI Marjorie Bowker's Response to John Crosbie's Letter

The Federal Government has issued a rebuttal to my analysis of the Free Trade Agreement. I am delighted that this has happened. It indicates that dialogue which has been lacking for so long with government may at last be emerging. The fact that my commentary has been so eagerly grasped by people across Canada indicates the hunger of Canadians for facts presented in language they can readily understand. The public was entitled to such information from the government which supports the deal, and which should have been made available out of the $24 million budget it is using for the publicity and promotion.

If such information had been forthcoming from that source, there would have been no need or market for my analysis; nor would it have been so widely featured by newspaper columnists across Canada, including those of the Toronto Star, the Ottawa Citizen (four articles), the Calgary Herald, the Edmonton Journal (three articles); national radio programs (Cross-Country Check-up, As it Happens), CBC radio Edmonton, Calgary and Ottawa; and television programs in Toronto, Ottawa and Edmonton.

Yes, the groundswell across Canada has been staggering - beyond anything I could have imagined or anticipated. Requests for copies of my analysis received at the office of Print 2000 in Ottawa have been in the hundreds daily. I am grateful to the proprietor of that office for providing copies for the public at a cost of $4.00. Every other expense has been borne by personally by choice. Perhaps it has taken this public outburst to touch the nerve of officials in the Federal Government. At least they mustered top personnel in the trade office to compile a rebuttal.

They point out my error in mixing "wine" and "spirit" in regard to timing of removal of discriminatory price mark-ups. I thank them for the correction. They take exception to my remarks on energy. If clarification is needed, my comments relate precisely to times of shortage, which could occur in the mid-1990's. They say the "national treatment" does not apply to workers: this is not what Article 1402 says. They say that the dispute settlement mechanism is binding. My response is that no decision or ruling is binding without sanctions to ensure enforcement and compliance. Termination and retaliation are punitive rather than measures of specific performance.

I thank the Federal Government for its thoughtful rebuttal. It does not alter my thesis that this is a bad deal for Canada. To conclude, I do not pretend to be the last word on this vast subject. I hope that other Canadians will prepare commentaries of their own and thereby contribute to the national debate. My goal will have been fulfilled, if, as a result of my analysis people do more thinking and talking. I am happy to have been a catalyst for dialogue on this vital issue relating to our country's future. I leave it to others to continue the debate.

Editor's Note:
The following section includes some of the articles
that appeared in newspapers across Canada, when
the original manuscript was released. Some of the
concerns expressed in these articles have been
incorporated into changes in the text of this revised
edition. The conclusions of the author remain
unaltered. There were many more articles that we
did not have enough space to reproduce. There
were only two articles, that we know of, negative to
the author's study. Both of these have been
included.

Media Responses

The following is a partial list of radio and television programs that were aired recently on the subject:

Radio:
> CBC Edmonton, August 31st;
> CBC Calgary, Sept. 1st;
> CBC "Canada News" from Toronto Sept. 1st;
> CBC "Cross Country Check-up" with The
>   Honorable John Crosbie as guest, Sept. 4;
> CBC "As it Happens", Sept. 5th;
> CBO Ottawa 90-minute special call-in morning
>   program, Sept. 15th;
> Q101-FM Smith Falls, Ontario, Sept. 19;
> CKLQ, Brandon, Manitoba, telephone open-line
>   program, October 5th.
> CBC National Radio, "Commentary",
>   October 11th, a three minute survey of The
>   Free Trade Agreement.

Television:

CTV Edmonton "Day by Day" Sept. 6th;
CBC National News, 10 p.m. with Wendy Mesley,
    Sept. 16th;
Two 6 o'clock newscasts on separate Ottawa channels
    Sept. 15;
CTV national "Question Period" (Pamela Wallin) (half-
    hour interview) - Sept. 18.

MEDIA RESPONSES

Former Judge Finds Much To Fear In Free Trade Pact.

THE TORONTO STAR
Sunday, July 31, 1988
Jim Coutts

Jim Coutts a Toronto Management consultant, was principle secretary to former prime minister Pierre Trudeau from 1975 to 1981.

Marjorie Bowker has read the U.S.-Canada free trade agreement and the massive legislative text now before Parliament that would bring the deal into being. Not only has she read it, she has followed the negotiation of the deal in detail, documented statements by public officials in both countries, looked at the pros and cons for Canada, and summarized her analysis in a 60-page brief that should be urgent reading for all Canadians.

So who is Marjorie Bowker? Well if you lived in Northern Alberta, you wouldn't have to ask. A law graduate from the University of Alberta, she practised in a leading Edmonton firm before being appointed a Family Court judge-a position she held for 17 years. She has championed the cause of women and is one of t brighter people in this country. As is clear from her brief, she brooks no nonsense with those who generally favor a trade deal even if they're not sure what it entails.

Her concerns about the free trade agreement developed as she heard ordinary citizens in Western Canada say they didn't understand what it was all about but they assumed it was deserving of their support. This worry was compounded when ministers responsible bragged they hadn't read the legislation they were steering through Parliament. Finally, when provincial politicians praised aspects of the deal that seemed certain to work against the interests of her native province, she decided it was time for action.

Bowker did what she had trained herself and others over a lifetime to do: read the document, get the facts, avoid the rhetoric, and try to discover just what the agreement means. Without outside funding and with no partisan axe to grind, she spells out the likely implications flowing from the most sweeping document ever to confront Canadians. She doesn't like what she sees and pulls no punches in spelling out her reasons.

The Bowker document is a timely piece. With the Mulroney government pressing full speed ahead with passage of the legislation and John Turner throwing a Senate crowbar into the parliamentary machine, we face a fall crisis and probably an election over the issue. It is rather useful that someone should take the time to read the bill.

Bowker begins with a bias that expanding our trade makes sense. But after her detailed review, she concludes that we are paying too high a price to eliminate the tariffs on the 20 per cent of goods that are now subject to duty between the U.S. and Canada. She explains what the words in the 200 pages of text mean.

She highlights the fact that Canada will be forced to sell fixed portions of our national resources - minerals, oil and gas - even, and especially, during periods when there are shortages here. She sees a real threat to Canadian agriculture and a real possibility of water diversion from Canada to the United States. And rather than creating massive numbers of new jobs, she exposes the likelihood of American service industries expanding into Canada and bringing U.S. citizens with them to fill the newly created positions.

She explains how specific sections of the agreement encourage even more takeover of Canadian industries and she deplores the lack of consumer protection for Canadians from U.S. financial institutions that will operate here. The cold hard facts of the bill before Parliament show American banks in Canada will have less stringent capital requirements and, unlike Canadian banks, need no approval to open additional branches. She deals as well with the changes that allow U.S. companies to begin to bid on Canadian government contracts.

Bowker summarizes well the likely impact of our technical standards having to be compatible with those in the United States. She shows by example that we could be forced to accept goods that might be environmentally unacceptable to us, but could not be kept out because our standards would be interpreted as a "barrier to trade." Even more frightening is her warning that our social legislation in health, pensions, unemployment insurance and workers' compensation will be interpreted as unfair subsidies.

The analysis looks at the impact of the law on particular industries and deals at great length with textiles, wine, autos and especially the oil and gas industry that is so critical to Alberta.

After looking in detail at the clauses governing dispute resolution and termination provisions, Bowker concludes we have a very bad deal on our hand. She acknowledges that many provisions that apply to Canada also apply to the united States. But the effects are not equal. The purpose of her commentary is to assess what happens to Canada. Too much is negative, she argues.

All of this she does without personal insult or political barb. Just the facts. She concludes the bill brings about economic union, not freer trade. Canadians ought to know about this before it's too late.

She's A Free-Trade Thinker For The Average Citizen

THE OTTAWA CITIZEN
Wednesday, August 31, 1988
Roy MacGregor

All through the day on Tuesday, all through the speech in favor by the prime minister and the speeches against by the leaders of the opposition, 72-year-old Marjorie Bowker sat patiently at the desk in her Edmonton home.

She was waiting, she says, for her own thoughts on free trade to "crystallize."

She had not interest in the vote that was coming up in the House of Commons because, in her studied opinion, the outcome has long been "a foregone conclusion."

What Marjorie Bowker of Edmonton is waiting so patiently for is the election call, when she is convinced the only vote that matters on free trade will be taken.

And she has been ready for that call for weeks.

To the side of Marjorie Bowker's desk are 200 fresh-printed copies of a remarkable document. It's title is straightforward - What Will The Free-Trade Agreement Mean To You And To Canada? - and she has typed at the bottom of this 58-page anaysis a small note that tells you something of her own personality: "Kindly Circulate."

She is a grandmother six times over, but is also a lawyer and, for 17 years, she sat as a judge of the Provincial Court of Alberta before retiring to her Edmonton home five years ago.

She had, she decided this June, precisely the qualifications needed for an average citizen's investigation into the free-trade deal.

"Something was happening to my country," she says in her matter-of-fact style, "and I wanted to find out what. It was the sort of thing no one could undertake unless you have a lot of time -

which I happen to have - and, if I may be permitted to say so, a fair degree of competence." Without the legal training, she says she would have abandoned the project almost instantly. "The Free Trade Agreement is abstract and ambiguous," she says. "It's filled with convoluted language and its implications are hidden."She began and ended her project as a supporter of freer trade, but she does not, as you may by now suspect think much of the document the prime minister spent so much of Tuesday praising.

"Ten of the 21 chapters have nothing to do with trade at all," she says. "They focus on economic union with the United States."

And while a column of this length can do no justice to her frank and accessible analysis, what she has seen in those now-familiar words has disturbed her greatly. Marjorie Bowker sees Canadians going for free trade convinced they will have more money in the pocket to spend on cheaper consumer goods.

Unfortunately, she cannot locate in free trade the jobs which would put the money in the pockets in the first place.

Canadian branch plants will close first, she believes. Second, other Canadians plants that cannot compete will collapse. And third, successful Canadian plants will become the prime targets of take-overs, leading to further plant closures as larger operations consolidate where the market, the money and the preferred labor pool is found.

She is further convinced that the final legal interpretation of the section that deals with resource industries will mean that, contrary to all those government assurances, Canada will not be able to control her own resources. As for oil and gas, she has two warnings for her fellow Albertans.

First, she believes the document legally binds a fixed proportion of Canadians energy to the Americans, even if Canada one day runs short. "We must still share our short supply with the U.S.," she writes, "however small that may be."

Secondly, she believes the agreement is written so that Canada is obliged to sell to the Americans at a price equal to or less that that of either U.S. or world producers.

On and on her relentless analysis moves until, by page 56, Marjorie Bowker has come to the conclusion that "Canada could face the eventual loss of political independence, and of its sovereignty as a nation." Beginning today, she will be addressing the 200 copies of her analysis to send it off to anyone she thinks might pass her warning on in a helpful manner.

It costs $1.48 to mail each one of her crystallized thoughts.

And she's hoping for delivery before the real vote begins.

Bowker's Medicare-is-doomed Thesis On Free Trade Nonsense

THE OTTAWA CITIZEN September 20, 1988, John Ferguson

If you get your appendix removed in the United States, the surgeon who puts you under the knife will be paid, on average, about $1,000.

In Canada, it will be closer to $400.

Your appendix won't know the difference. And you'll heal no more quickly in the U.S. than in Canada.

The big difference is that physicians earn a lot more in the U.S. because medicine there is simply another business, whereas in Canada, it's virtually all state controlled. That means governments negotiate fee schedules and that keeps prices down.

Add in the high cost of liability insurance in the U.S. - more than $100,000 per physician - and the fact that there are more doctors per capital and you've got the makings of a very costly and inefficient system south of the border.

That's why scare stories suggesting medicate and other social programs are threatening by free trade are nonsense. By any objective measure, Canada has a less costly, fairer and more efficient medical system because we have simply decided, as a nation to spread the costs across the entire population.

As a result total health care costs are nearly a third less per capita in Canada than in the U .S.

In 1985, Canadian's total spending on health care totalled about 8.5 per cent of Gross Domestic Product (GDP) compared with 10.7 per cent in the U.S.

And we do this while providing health coverage for virtually 100 per cent of the population. In the U.S., 36 million people have no medical insurance and it's estimated another 50 million have inadequate coverage for a serious or prolonged illness. Average life span is longer and infant mortality rates are lower in Canada, two measures of the quality of health care.

One of the proponents of the "medicare is doomed" thesis has been Marjorie Bowker, the retired family court judge whose simplistic and too-often inaccurate analysis of the free trade deal has been promoted in the media as a down-to-earth guide to free trade for the layman.

The Bowker thesis, which has been pushed by others opposed to the deal, is that medicare and other social programs would be considered subsidies and "unfair trade practices" and would be used as an excuse to slap countervailing duties on Canadian imports into the U.S.

This ignores the fact that the principle is clearly established in U.S. trade law that government programs that are widely available, as opposed to those targeted at a single industry to assist its exports, cannot be made subject to countervailing duties.

Bowker, also argues, contradicting her first point, that Canadian companies will put pressure on Canadian governments to eliminate costly social programs which drive up costs. She thinks it will drive investment south of the border.

So we are asked to believe that our social programs will make our companies too competitive in the U.S. and get slapped with countervailing duties at the same time as they make us less competitive and cause Canadian companies to pressure governments to eliminate them.

The arguments cancel each other and suggest Bowker should stick to family law, not international trade law and economics.

If wage costs and payroll taxes were the major factor on plant location, all of U.S. industry would shift to the U.S. sunbelt where there are no minimum wages.

In Canada, it's mainly the low-wage industries which are sensitive to payroll taxes used to help fund social programs such as unemployment insurance and the Canadian Pension Plan.

These tend to be concentrated in the service sector - restaurants, shoe stores and the like - which are not vulnerable under the free trade in any case because they aren't transportable.

As for medical care, the U.S. should be adopting our system.

It would make their economy more efficient.

Canadians Are Hungry For Facts On Trade Deal

THE OTTAWA CITIZEN
Tuesday, September 6, 1988
Marjorie Nichols

Those politicians who believe that the average Canadian voter is a bubblehead, unable or unwilling to grapple with complex issues such as the Canadian-U.S. free-trade agreement, could be in for a rude surprise.

Indeed, if the experience of my fellow columnist Roy Mac-Gregor is indicative, the pollsters are dead wrong about free trade.

MacGregor, at 40 a veteran of this business, is still shaking his head in disbelief at what happened last week. So are the rest of us who share a downtown Sparks Street office with him.

Briefly, MacGregor smacked out a good, but otherwise ordinary column last Wednesday about a 72-year-old Edmonton woman who has prepared a 58 page analysis of the free-trade agreement.

The woman, Marjorie Montgomery Bowker, is not an ordinary Canadian. She is a lawyer and retired judge and her analysis of the trade treaty is brilliant.

She has taken this complicated document, which even the responsible minister admits he hasn't read, and reduced it to a layman's level with a clarity of language to make any ink-stained wretch drool. These are, of course, exactly the qualities that distinguish great judicial opinion: clarity of thought, language and reason.

Bowker, with true judicial impartiality, declares her personal interest. It is, simply, to spread enlightment.

As she puts it: "What impelled the writer to undertake this analysis were widespread comments from even the most educated Canadians that they do not understand what the free-trade agreement is all about." But to get back to MacGregor, who was first told about the Bowker paper two weeks ago by a political friend.

MacGregor didn't think about the matter again until last Tuesday when he remembered the call and the story and figured it might provide the ingredients for a column.

Shortly after Wednesday's paper hit the street, it started: the deluge of telephone calls. Everyone with a subscription to the Citizen, it seemed, wanted MacGregor to get them a copy of Marjorie Bowker's free-trade analysis. No one kept an exact count of the calls. They were still coming in Friday when MacGregor reckoned that he had received about 110.

At the reception desk inside our downtown office - Suite 805 at 165 Sparks St. - we have installed a huge sign and a sort of lend-lease library. Citizens who want a copy of Marjorie Bowker's work are invited to take MacGregor's original, run down the street to a copying shop, make some copies and then return the original.

I'm guessing that there may be a newspaper columnist somewhere in this country who had generated more interest in a serious topic. But I don't know when or where. Neither does MacGregor.

He says that no column he has ever written came even close to generating such a landslide of interest.

"I didn't even get this kind of interest after Otto Lang sued me for criminal libel."

MacGregor figures that he, like the pollsters and the politicians, had "completely misread the average Canadian...I've just completely changed my mind. And I feel like a real fool." I'll have to apply for membership in the fool's club as well.

MacGregor points out another astonishing thing, which is that those who have been lining up at our door aren't public service mandarins or industry monguls.

They are truly average Canadians. As MacGregor puts it: "At least 98 per cent of them are ordinary people...retired couples from Perth and Alymer and Cobden and a lot of other people who ride the bus to work."

He's also incredulous at something else. A number of those who have trudged down to our office to make copies of MacGregor's copy of Marjorie Bowker's work have called back to say thanks. And that, believe me, is mighty unusual.

Are Ottawans any different from other average Canadians? Somehow, I doubt it. I think that Marjorie Bowker is what ordinary Canadians have been looking for: an impartial source who can assist them in making one of the most important decisions of their voting lives.

Makes you kind of proud to be a Canadian, doesn't it?

OPINION
Trade Bluster
Clouds Reality

The Edmonton Journal
Wednesday, August,31, 1988

Bluster and bombast are poor substitutes for rational analysis and thoughtful debate.

Yet even as the Commons debate on free trade drew to a close, John Crosbie - the minister responsible for shepherding the agreement through Parliament - abandoned reason for rhetoric.

Crosbie says the Liberals are "criminally negligent" in their attack on the free-trade deal.

Is the minister any less so in his refusal to promote the substance of the treaty? Consumed by partisan zeal, Crosbie chooses to attack his critics rather than defend the trade pact on its merits.

As the House of Commons prepares to send to Senate Bill C-130, the free-trade enabling legislation, Canadians should understand that the Mulroney trade deal is riddled with flaws.

Many Canadians have studied the agreement and identified potential problems. One recent and unsettling analysis comes from retired Alberta judge Marjorie Bowker.

One of the cornerstones is access to the U.S. market. Yet Bowker shows that Canada remains subject to American countervailing duties, the principle barrier to free trade.

And when it comes to the so-called "binding" method of settling disputes, the learned judge finds it anything but.

To be binding in a legal sense, she says, any dispute-settlement "requires remedies or sanctions to redress breaches, and assure compliance. By no reasonable interpretation does the free-trade agreement provide this. Without binding mechanism for settlement of disputes, any agreement is rendered impotent."

Bowker's analysis certainly is not the Liberal "arrogance" Crosbie huffs about. The judge makes it clear that she is a free trader - she simply believes that this deal is flawed, poorly constructed and bad for Canada. Exactly.

Ottawa should abandon its arrogance and amend the free-trade deal to reflect Canada's best interests.

Four-fifths of our trade with the U.S. already is free. We have made scant gains to free the remainder, while giving up a large measure of our sovereignty. The loss of sovereignty comes not just in the implied culture threat some Canadians speak of but in a very real legal sense.

Bowker notes that the free-trade legislation supersedes a host of federal statutes that are critical to sovereignty, from the Bank Act to the Income Tax Act to the National Energy Board Act.

The legislation "contains sweeping revisions of Canadian stature law, on a scale unprecedented in a single act - including wherever necessary an encroachment on provincial powers."

Any reasonable Canadian would be moved to reflection by such an analysis. Are Crosbie and his prime minister prepared to be reasonable?

Here's The Beef

Edmonton Journal Editorial
September 14, 1988

In bringing substance to the free-trade debate, Marjorie Bowker had succeeded where the opposition has failed.

The retired Edmonton judge has lifted the free-trade debate from a rhetorical rut with a sharp and measured analysis that has brought quick government response.

Agree or disagree with Bowker, Canadians ought to thank her for a belated opportunity to argue the sum and substance of the Canada-U.S. Free Trade Agreement.

For too long, the Mulroney government's trade deal has been painted by each side's huckster as (a) our salvation, or (b) our destruction.

Reasonable Canadians expect to find the truth in between, and Bowker's analysis provokes the thoughtful debate that will lead to more measured and honest opinions.

For the first time International Trade Minister John Crosbie is responding to the substance of the argument.

This is far preferable to the previous tactic of pushing the principle of free trade while avoiding scrutiny of the deal itself.

Even so, Crosbie's answers lack conviction. He tries to downplay Bowker's concern about American access to Canadian energy by saying it applies only in "very limited circumstances."

And what are these "very limited circumstances?" Oh, you know, the minor stuff. Like when Canada runs short of oil and wants to ensure it has enough for domestic needs. As Crosbie puts it, "where a government imposes export restrictions for reasons of conservation, short supply or domestic price stabilization."

He'll need better answers if he hopes to rebut Bowker's coolly devastating analysis. But at least he's trying to answer. And that's good news for everyone who wants the facts rather than the hype on free trade.

Lion Of The Day Lacks Credibility

THE MONTREAL GAZETTE
September 20, 1988
William Johnson

OTTAWA - It is a sign of the times that Marjorie Bowker, a retired family court judge in Alberta - someone used to dealing with alimony, delinquency, disputes between spouses, and the like - has been promoted to chief standard-bearer of the anti-free-trade- movement.

"She has no axe to grind: she simply speaks the truth," said an editorial yesterday in The Gazette.

Personally, I'm glad Bowker found time in her retirement to produce the analysis. She could well start a trend for the golden age. Perhaps we can expect an in-depth analysis of the Meech Lake accord by a retired United Church minister, an analysis of the child-care legislation by a retired detective, a thorough investigation Bill C-136 (the broadcasting Act) by a retired band leader and - why not? - an analysis of the Bank of Canada's monetary policy by a retired show salesman.

With the progressive aging of the population, euchre and square dancing clearly will not do to keep us all busy. Bowker, now one of the country's best known senior citizens, has pioneered a whole new concept. She showed that the press will lionize a grandmother who bites government.

Haven't studied critique

I haven't really studied Bowker's 60-page negative critique, only sampled paragraphs of her opus here and there for the flavour. In a world of wonders, with so much to learn and so little time, with life so short - at least, until I, too, get to retirement to launch my 60-page grenades on all the problems of the day - I prefer to devote the availabe hours to reading authors with more credible credentials.

For instance, it seems to me that the just-released Survey of Canada by the Paris-based Organization for Economic Co-operation and Development (OECD), which includes all the major industrialized countries, had some claim to the attention of Canadians.

The OECD reviewed the evience of the likely impact of the free-trade agreement as projected by economic studies.

"All studies suggest significant gains from free trade," the OECD said in its report.

"An important feature of the gains is that they are generated by economies of scale."

"The earlier experience of the United States-Canada Automobile Pact demonstrated the importance of scale effects: Indeed, the marked improvement in productivity that occurred in the years following the pact was due in large part to economies of scale. The Canadian industry not only closed the productivity gap but has become more efficient than American plants, on account of more modern capital equipment."

The OECD's favorable judgment on the Canada-U.S. free trade agreement did not attract much attention, unlike Bowker's solo flight, simply because it represents the well-known consensus of the great majority of economists, of most of the heads of state (as indicated by the approval at the June Toronto meeting of the Group of Seven heads), of eight of the 10 premiers.

Large economic benefits

"Canada is expected to derive large economic benefits from such liberalization," the OECD continues.

"The agreement is expected to

result in lower consumer prices, expanded market opportunities and greater efficiency for the realization of economics of scale."

But what is the best judgment, admittedly fallible, of the OECD in comparison with "the truth" spoken by a Marjorie Bowker?

It is a telling commentary on the anti-free-trade case - long on emotion,short on economic analysis - that a person with no particular expertise in the subject should become an instant guru, lionized by anti-free-traders from coast to coast.

It indicates that the credibility and expertise of those attacking the agreement can't compare with the credibility of its defenders - including a royal commission by Donald Macdonald; several reports by the Economic Council of Canada; the country's leading economists, such as Richard Lipsey; and its most reputable think-tanks, including the C.D. Howe Institute and the Institute for research on Public Policy.

But what is all that compared to one grandmother who shouts: "The free-trade agreement has no clothes"?

Letters To The Editor
Montreal Gazette
September 26, 1988

More to Canada than Economics
Andrew Allen

William Johnson Gratuitously condescending comments on the opinions of Marjorie Bowker (Comment, Sept 20, "Lion of the Day Lacks Credibility") seem to be summed up in his final sentence "But what is all that to one Grandmother who shouts 'The free trade has no clothes'.?"

Has he not overlooked the essence of the fable that it was just one child among a throng of "betters" who voiced the truth?

He might, too, have been more careful in his tentative acceptance of the opinion of some economists. Two such recently wrote to the Times of London to explain how 364 "present or retired members of the economics staff of British Universities" could have been so wrong seven years ago in unanimously condemning government policies which they said would " deepen the depression, erode the industrial base of (the U.K.) economy and threaten its social and political stability"

Whether or not this near

unanimity proves to be right or wrong, surely the principal basis for doubt about the free trade treaty lies in the far broader field of Canadian Social or cultural affairs. There is more to Canada than economics.

Never Had Marbles To Lose?
C.H. McGuire

I admire your columnist William Johnson for his writing ability and his facility for pinpointing an obviously stupid point of view. However, he goes too far in The Gazette of Sept. 20.

Like Marjorie Bowker, I can also find time in my retirement (I am 85 years old) to criticize the free-trade deal and Mr. Johnson. I am quite aware of the fact that many older people have "lost their marbles," but it is equally true that many younger people never had any to lose.

The free-trade deal is not a subject reserved for economists and businessmen. It is much more farreaching than that. What Mr. Johnson cannot see is that there are two sides to it, the economic side and the more general quality of life side.

Our society and many others are too prone to value everything in terms of money and what money can buy. The other day, I was arguing free trade with my younger brother and he accused me of being blind to the real issue because I had never been a businessman. I agreed, of course, that I did not have the businessman's outlook, but I was grateful having a broader outlook than that.

If Marjorie Bowker is a grandmother who, in Mr. Johnson's words, shouts, "The free trade agreement had no clothes," I would reply that the average economist and businessman has tunnel vision.

Not Qualified?
James I. Gow

What a despicable column by William Johnson (Gazette, Sept.20, "Lion of the day lacks credibility").

He says that retired people are not qualified to comment on the great public issues of the day. Good Heavens, incompetence has not kept Mr. Johnson from pontificating on all kinds of issues.

Target Wasn't Grandmother But Media That Lionized Her

MONTREAL GAZETTE
William Johnson

OTTAWA - That's the last time I beat up on a 72-year old grandmother.

My Sept. 20 column on Marjorie Bowker and her analysis of the Canada-U.S. free-trade agreement has brought me more angry reaction than anything I've ever written.

Usually I feel professional satisfaction if a column of mine, expressing my true views, elicits anger, indignation, outrage, even ridicule and abuse.

A case in point is a column I wrote on the death of chansonnier Félix Leclerc. It stated that he had incited hatred against English in Quebec, and the column provoked many angry letters, including one missive which particularly delighted me.

Someone had cut out the column, drawn a square around the photo of my head and inscribed the caption "Tête carrée " (a Quebec slang term for anglos is square-head). The artist eddied for good measure: "Pauve cul," and signed it "MLQ" - presumable standing for the Movement for the liberation of Quebec.

The informed and civil reaction of indignation as well as the scurrilous anonymous hate mail convinced me that what I had said needed saying. No regrets there.

But the reaction to the columnon Marjorie Bowker has me on the run, Mea culpa, I surrender. Hereby follows my abject apology.

The column was taken by many as ridiculing senior citizens and the retired. Or as putting down Marjorie Bowker's analysis of free-trade agreement because it was written by a non-expert.

With exemplary à propos James Gow (Letters, Sept.30) wrote this from Westmount:

"What a despicable column by William Johnson. He says that retired people are not qualified to comment on the great public issues of the day Good heavens, incompetence has not kept Mr.Johnson from pontificating on all kinds of issues.

The final straw came when my 83-year-old mother told me, "No more cookies for you."

The most offensive sentences in the column were these - if recalling them doesn't risk putting the other foot in my mouth:

"Perhaps we can expect an indepth analysis of the Meech Lake accord by a retired United Church minister, an analysis of the child-care legislation by a retired detective, a thorough investigation of Bill C-136 (the Broadcasting Act) by a retired band leader and - why not? - an analysis of the Bank of Canada's monetary policy by a retired shoe sales-man.

"With the progressive aging of the population, euchre and square dancing clearly will not do to keep us all busy, Bowker, now one of the country's best known senior citizens, has pioneered a whole new concept. She showed that the press will lionize a grandmother who bites government."

In my defence, be it made clear that I do not think people become less intellectually competent as they get older. On the contrary: 57 years old myself, I truely believe that I am a better critic now than I was 10 years ago, but not as good as I'll be 10 years from now. Why would it be different for others?

Nor do I think retired people incompetent. Personally, once retired from daily journalism, it's my intention to write books - to take advantage of financial security without the daily demands so as to undertake more ambitious and less ephemeral writing project.

Nor do I think the non-expert to be disqualified from commenting on the free-trade agreement or any other issue of public significance.

On the contrary, as James Gow perspicaciously pointed out, a columnist like me is precisely a generalist who earns a living by commenting, day by day, on issues of importance to other ordinary citizens.

What, then,was the point of my criticism and of my badly executed satire? It was contained in the first paragraph of the offensive column.

"It is a sign of the times that Marjorie Bowker, a retired family court judge in Alberta - someone used to dealing with alimony, delinquency, disputes between spouses, and the like - has been promoted to chief standard-bearer of the anti-free-trade movement.

I have no quarrel with Marjorie Bowker. My quarrel is with those who lionized her, made her into an oracle.

"She has no axe to grind; she simply speaks the truth," The Gazette, resolutely against the free-trade agreement, said in an editorial.

Now, I have a great deal of re spect for Donald Macdonald, who chaired the Royal Commission on the Economic Union and Development Prospects for Canada. A man of great intelligence and great integrity, he acquired experience in many cabinet portfolios, including as minister of energy and minister of finance. He then spent years pondering Canada's future as head of the royal commission, and benefited from the research and the advice of the best brains in the country.

He recommended free trade with the United States! His recommendation should carry some weight. But still, I would never write something as uncritical as "he speaks the truth."

Marjorie Bowker herself was much more modest when she appeared on CTV's Question Period.

"Really I prepared this, more than anything else, for my education.

"I didn't know - I'm an ordinary Canadian, so initially it began as an effort on my part to comprehend, really, what this was. I felt that if it was something that was going to effect my country, maybe I should know - and it expanded beyond that, really, because of the constant comments I was hearing from people: 'Really I wish I knew more about it.'

"So that's why I just put it together."

We need many more Marjorie Bowkers. But they don't need or want to be turned by th news media into oracles.

Tories Rebut Free-Trade Tract Written By Retired Judge

THE OTTAWA CITIZEN
Tuesday, September 13,1988

The federal government, apparently stung by a free-trade critique written by a 72-year-old retired family court judge, has written a derogatory rebuttal.

A paper prepared by the trade-negotiations office calls the free-trade analysis by Marjorie Bowker of Edmonton a "pseudo-legal analysis" that's riddles with errors.

"In many instances. she simply does not know what she is talking about," says the unsigned report from the trade office, which worked out the free-trade deal with the United States last fall.

Bowker has granted requests for newspaper, television and national radio interviews since her 59-page, photocopied booklet was released in July on a $1,000 budget. The booklet is titled What Will The Free Trade Mean To You And To Canada?

She said she has been receiving 20 calls a day at her home requesting copies of her booklet, which concludes that the benefits of free-trade are outweighed by the costs to Canadian sovereignty.

Meanwhile business is brisk for the Ottawa printer selling copies of the report.

Michael Kanstrup, manager of Print 2000, estimated he has had 600 inquiries since last week. By Saturday, he had sold between 300 and 400 copies of the booklet at his Bank Street location.

Bowker said she stands by her analysis.

FREE TRADE : Are Canadians Giving Away Too Much?

THE MIRROR
September 19, 1988
High Prairie
Kerri Gnass

Eighty per cent of trade between Canada and the United States is free of tariffs and duties. Hence, the Free Trade Agreement deals with only the remaining 20 per cent of trade between the two countries.

Retired judge Marjorie Bowker, in a detailed analysis of the agreement released last month, poses this question: Are Canadians giving away too much for the sake of 20 per cent?

As far as world trade, Statistics Canada figures show that for the first four months of 1988, Canada had been running at a surplus of $800 million per month-- which works out to an annual trade surplus of $9,6 billion.

In contrast, for the month of May, the United States had a world trade deficit of $10 billion. "A one-month U.S. deficit exceeds Canada's yearly surplus," Bowker points out.

"In other words," she says, "Who needs it (free trade) most? Who will benefit most?

Bowker is convinced that what Canada has given away to clear the remaining 20 per cent of trade barriers is "enormous", and questions the soundness of entering an "economic union" with a country that has become the word's greatest debtor and is expected to have a national debt of $13 trillion by the year 2000.

Bowker says the declining influence of the U.S. on world economy, and the fact that Japan has now exceeded the States in it's gross national product and is expected to become the world's largest economy, must be considered.

As well, Canada and the United States are already each other's biggest customers, buying and selling $150 billion worth of goods and services annually.

Does Canada need to pursue even freer trade with the U.S.?

Marjorie Bowker says no.

"A better option for Canada is to develop multi-national trade

On Guard For Thee   123

relationships, especially with countries in the Pacific," she concludes.

Free-Trade Deal As Clear As Mud

SOUTHAM NEWS
September 16, 1988
(Circulated to newspapers across Canada)
Don McGillivray

OTTAWA - Canadians want to know more about the free-trade deal before they vote on it.

In the latest government poll, 72 per cent of the sample answered no to this question: "Do you feel you understand the issue as well as you would like?"

The government's response has been a crude and clumsy propaganda campaign, not designed to clarify the issue but to stampede the voters into voting Conservative. Using tax money for this partisan purpose was highly questionable.

Public thirst for more information has been highlighted by the rush to get copies of the 60-page photocopied analysis by Marjorie Bower. The 72-year-old retired Alberta provincial-court judge did her study because of "widespread comments from even the most educated Canadians that

they do not understand what the free-trade is all about."

Her analysis probably has holes in it. It would be strange if it didn't. But the reaction of the government shows how jumpy it is about free trade.

The Trade Negotiations Office, which worked out the deal with the U.S., tried to squash Bowker with an eight-page release claiming her analysis is "riddled with errors of interpretation."

Trade Minister John Crosbie has jumped on her with all the weight of hes office. He's been writing letters to newspapers to rebut her conclusions.

And Informetrica, an Ottawa think-tank quoted Wednesday by the Mulroney government side of the Senate free-trade debate, complained in its regular newsletter that the media were making a "star" of Bowker.

This seems a ridiculous overreaction.

Tories may have developed an inordinate fear of retired women in 1985 when Solange Denis, a pensioner protesting de-indexation, confronted the prime minister and told him, "You lied to us. You made us vote for you then goodbye. Goodbye Charlie Brown."

Whatever the reason, the episode shows the government anxious to demolish rather than applaud people who try to figure out the trade deal on their own.

As Crosbie says in his letter, we're supposed to get our information from government propaganda booklets obtained by phoning the official telephone numbers. We're not supposed to try to do it on our own.

Most of the economic think tanks have been wise enough to reach the official conclusions. It's easy. You tell the computer what to think and it turns your assumptions into fact.

But the thank-tank studies are as full of holes as Bowker's do-it-yourself effort. They say present industries won't flee Canada under free trade. But they take little or no account of future plant location.

Suppose you were a corporate executive trying to decide where to locate a new plant under free trade.

You confront a North American market of 270 million consumers of whom 244 million are in one country and 26 million in another. All things being equal, you'd probably locate in the larger part of the market.

If you located in Canada, a rise in the Canadian dollar would raise your costs in American dollars, in which most of your output would have to be sold.

This trend to locate in the U.S. rather than Canada is already evident in what Maclean's magazine calls "a race to invest in America."

The cover story on "the economic integration of Canada and the U.S." quotes one Canadian investor in the U.S. : "Americans won't give you a large percentage of their money if you're situated in Canada."

This sort of thing has never been analysed by the pom-pom crew cheering the trade deal.

We should know more about it before we vote for it.

To Critics Of The Author's Credibility

Although attacks have been few, they deserve to be addressed. It might clarify their bases.

Is it because my chosen specialty throughout my judicial career has been in the field of family law; child abuse; juvenile delinquency and marriage breakdown (even though I have been married for 48 years)? A lawyer becomes a specialist only after being a generalist.

Is it the fact that I am a woman? That would be strange, as I have never perceived or experienced this as as discriminatory factor in my lifetime's activities.

Or is it because people have somehow come to see me as a hero because I have given them something they wanted and which they could understand? If so, it is far from the first time in my life that I have been unseekingly acclaimed for things I happen to have done in the legal or humanitarian field.

My interest in study and analysis is nothing new. I have made an oral and written presentation at public hearing on the Meech Lake Accord (September 1987); a brief to the Premier's Commission on Alberta's Future Health Care (February 1988); and a commentary and petition on the United Church Sexuality Report (May 1988).

And I do at last have time to reflect on the myriad of current issues confronting our country, some national importance.

As for expertise, if I haven't acquired some of that through my experiences, I must indeed be a dullard. These years of retirement, I perceive as the "bonus years of life". I hope my critics will enjoy theirs as I am enjoying mine. Long ago I learned this proverb: If you do something important, there will always be critics. If you don't like critics, don't do anything important.

Marjorie M.Bowker

September 25, 1988.

On Guard For Thee

About The Author

Marjorie Montgomery Bowker was born in Prince Edward Island. Her father was a second cousin of Lucy Maud Montgomery. Raised in Alberta, she graduated in Arts and Law from the University of Alberta. She practised with an Edmonton law firm where she met her husband and has been married for forty-eight years.

In 1966 she was appointed a Judge of the Family and Juvenile Courts of Alberta, a position she held for seventeen years. While serving in that capacity, she was instrumental in establishing within the court system a Counselling and Conciliation Service aimed at preventing divorce, reducing divorce and conciliating differences created by divorce, which has become a model for other courts in Canada. In 1968 she was awarded an honorary degree of Doctor of Laws by Ewha Women's University in Seoul, Korea, on of the leading universities in Asia.

She has been a speaker at local, national and international gathering on a variety of topics including: "The Judicial System of Canada" (Seattle 1975); "The Role of Women in the Next Half Century" (Korea 1968); "Child Abuse" (Montreal 1977); "Can the Family Survive?" (Canadian Clubs across Canada and Canadian Forces Bases in West Germany 1979) and "The Meech Lake Constitutional Accord" (Edmonton 1987).

Since her retirement in 1983 she has had articles published in legal journals on subjects relating to Juvenile Court. She is also a volunteer in pastoral care at the University Hospital, Edmonton.

The Bowker are retired and active. They live in their home near the University campus in Edmonton. They have three children and six grandchildren.

Further Reading
After this analysis was completed in July 1988, a new book came to hand containing articles by 21 outstanding scholars from all parts of Canada. Their writings contain an analysis of all aspects of the Free Trade Agreement, and its impact upon Canada. Their conclusions are much more adverse to the Free Trade Agreement than is this analysis. Though the book is rather heavy reading, it leads one to conclude that the Free Trade Agreement will have a more devastating effect upon Canada than the public yet realizes. The name of this book is "The Free Trade Deal" Edited by Duncan Cameron, Professor of Political Economy, University of Ottawa.

On Guard For Thee